To: Penny,

Blessings as you weave the tapestry of your beautiful life. Keep making a difference.

Grace!
Janice Stockman

Underneath the Tapestry

A Collection of Inspiration from an Ordinary
Girl Who Serves an Extraordinary God

JANICE M. STOCKMAN

WESTBOW
PRESS®
A DIVISION OF THOMAS NELSON
& ZONDERVAN

WestBow Press books may be ordered through booksellers or by contacting:

WestBow Press
A Division of Thomas Nelson & Zondervan
1663 Liberty Drive
Bloomington, IN 47403
www.westbowpress.com
1 (866) 928-1240

ISBN: 978-1-4908-9196-5 (sc)
ISBN: 978-1-4908-9198-9 (hc)
ISBN: 978-1-4908-9197-2 (e)

Print information available on the last page.

WestBow Press rev. date: 10/01/2015

Introduction

This whole thing started because I turned 40. I guess maybe I never thought it would happen, but it snuck up on me. I toyed with writing a book for a long time but never could wrap my arms around my "voice". Did I want to write my life story......or a memoir of conversations in an educator's office......or simply provide some encouragement along the way for other weary travelers who are trying to make an impact on the world? The idea of "Underneath the Tapestry" started formulating and a certain friend kept encouraging me. Then, I started a blog and then a countdown "40 Days til 40" and I just kept writing.

I know it is not politically correct anymore to say that I love Jesus. However, I do. My faith is a huge part of who I am - not just what I do. If you are a person of faith, please hear my heart. If you are not, I pray you can find encouragement in these words and that they will seep in your heart and cause you to look up to the One who makes all the difference.

Acknowledgements

To the ladies (and the guys) who have encouraged me to write down my musings, thank you!!! You all believed in this project before I ever considered it a possibility. To my Sunday School classes, thank you for listening to my stories over the years. You will recognize some of them throughout these pages. You have all been a huge source of encouragement!

To the ladies who have helped edit, thank you! The five of you are absolutely incredible! I wish I had more to offer than a hearty thank you, a signed copy, and a big hug. You will never know the impact you have as you cultivate the seeds planted here!

To my inner circle - and you know who you are - there are simply no words to adequately express my gratitude. From the gentle nudging to the words of encouragement to the words that sharpen and are sometimes hard to hear, you have been exactly what I needed throughout this process. Thank you for helping me work through insecurities, for reading some days with tears in your eyes, and for loving me through this process. Your influence on my life is sprinkled throughout these pages, and I would never be the person I am today without you! I love each of you!

To Jeff, Carter & Cleveland, thank you. Without you, there would be far less stories to tell and a million memories missing from my life. You have loved, supported, and encouraged me beyond words. You love me the same on my best days and my worst days. I could never design a more perfect family for me. I love you immensely and am grateful God put me in this very spot! Thank you for making me laugh, for late night snuggles, and for indulging me in this crazy notion!

Most importantly, I would like to thank God for giving me a voice. Even if no one ever reads these pages, I have been able to articulate my relationship with Him in a way that has helped me grow and learn and see through to the heart of those around me.

This is dedicated to my granny, Edith Mary Hutchison. She has been in heaven for many years, and never knew of my desire to write while she was on this earth. But, this desire was born as a little girl reading the volumes of notebooks of poetry and songs she had written. I never fully appreciated her intimate relationship with God while she walked this earthly sod, but am thrilled she planted a seed in me all those years ago that has sprouted. I love you Granny!

Day 1

Underneath the Tapestry

VERSE: Isaiah 49:16: "See, I have engraved you on the palms of my hands; your walls are ever before me."

This is my testimony. I am the girl who sees my life from the wrong side of heaven.

A young girl sat at her grandmother's feet as she was embroidering. The little girl scampered around playing with paper dolls and a few legos. Every now and again she would look up at the material her grandmother was holding. She could not figure out what she was doing. There were strings everywhere and the colors seemed mismatched all over. She continued playing but continued wondering. After a while, she asked her grandmother what she was doing. The elderly grandmother told her she was creating a masterpiece. The little girl simply giggled - that made no sense, of course. She went back to playing.

One last time, she looked up at the material underneath with all the strings and all the knots. The wise grandmother could feel her curiosity. She waited only a moment longer and told the little girl to come sit by her and see the masterpiece. The little girl climbed on the floral sofa and was amazed at what she saw. It was simply breathtaking!

The grandmother explained that the thread had to criss-cross on the back so she could get it in the perfect place on the top side. When the thread ran out, she had to tie a knot so it could hold on. To create a beautiful picture, it took all colors of thread - sometimes in random places. At the end, it was perfect!

We get frustrated with our knots and criss-cross strings in life. Sometimes the patterns do not make sense. But, the problem is - we are looking at life from the wrong perspective. We are like the little girl playing with the activities of life, glancing up now and again to try to make sense of our circumstances. This side of heaven, life looks a little messy. It looks like there is no rhyme or reason to the patchwork we see. One day - one glorious day - we will meet our maker and we will see our life portrait in the art gallery and we will understand all the mixed-up colors and the knots. We will see that our tapestry is perfectly created with care and precision. And that will truly be a day that makes all the difference!

The challenge for today is that we remember our perspective - that we see underneath the tapestry of our lives. During times of criss-crossed threads and knots, let us not lose faith. Let us remember that we will understand those patterns one day as we trust the One who has our lives in the palm of His hand.

CHALLENGE: How often do I forget that I am looking underneath the tapestry? Why do I forget so easily?

Day 2

The Whisker

VERSE: 2 Corinthians 13:5: "Examine yourselves to see whether you are in the faith; test yourselves. Do you not realize that Christ Jesus is in you - unless, of course, you fail the test."

Most mornings, I am in a rush to get ready. It gets crazy! I have the same routine everyday – you would think that I would learn. But, day after day, I press the snooze button "one more time" and push morning activities to the last minute. I rush to get ready, to make sure snacks are packed, papers are signed, pants are ironed, and hair is combed. I know exactly what part of the morning news program must be playing when I brush my teeth to let me know if I am REALLY running behind. There are some mornings, albeit rare, that I wake up early and enjoy the process of readying for the day. The stress level is down and life seems so much more organized.

Such was the morning I did more than glance in the mirror. Then, I noticed it. That hair on the right side of my chin. Yes, THAT one. It sneaks up on me and I never notice it until it is embarrassing. Why can I not catch it when it is tiny???? So, I plucked it and went on about my day.

Except that little hair on my chinny-chin-chin bugged me all day long. My spiritual life is a lot like that. I tend to sing a few praise songs and lift up a few prayers and read a few verses. My walk with God has a general ebb and flow. But, the truth is that I rarely EXAMINE myself. Isn't that what the Word says?? "Examine yourself to see if you are in the faith." I tend to glance in the mirror of my spiritual life to see if everything appears in order. But, when I look a little more intensely, I often see a flaw – something that needs to be taken care of. Too often, my flaws, my insecurities, my sins, my shortcomings, my stumbling blocks – have to be long and wiggly before I notice them.

God wants me to examine myself daily so I can catch those flaws when they are tiny. My daily walk should be more than a passing glance – more than an "appearance" check – it should be a deep look so I can resemble Him more each day.

CHALLENGE: Why is it difficult to truly EXAMINE ourselves? Our walk with Christ be more than just for appearances. Take some time today to reflect on who you are and where your spiritual life stands.

Day 3

Man your post

VERSE: Romans 12:2: "Do not conform any longer to the pattern of this world, but be transformed by the renewing of your mind. Then you will be able to test and approve what God's will is - his good, pleasing and perfect will."

I love football season!!! There is nothing better than eating boiled peanuts wrapped up in my favorite blanket watching the Boys of Fall. I love the crispness in the air, the clash of shoulder pads, and the chants of the faithful. From junior high boys to the SEC in college football, my heart sings while watching a good game.

Watching ten-year-olds is entirely different. Maybe, it is that watching MY child is entirely different. I pace the stands, wring my hands, and sometimes cover my eyes and lift a silent prayer that he plays well. His playing football prompts many conversations at our house since my husband is also a junior high football coach.

Jeff has talked to our son many times about the position of outside linebacker (and similar jobs). I have heard him repeatedly say not to get "sucked in the middle". He tells the boy to man his post so that when the opponent comes around the outside, he is ready to tackle him. Last week at a game, I heard the opposing coach yelling from the sidelines, "Don't get sucked in!!!!" The spectator in me objects: that is where the action is!!!! Why not go where all the activity is? Coaches know, however, that if the outside linebacker ends up in the middle, there is no one to cover the running back. The coach reminds them over and over. You would think these boys would learn to stay put and man their post. Why is it so hard to stay out of all the activity in the middle?

The same is true for Christians. It is difficult to be "set apart". It is much easier to be in the middle of the hustle and bustle and all the activities that life has to offer. The truth is – God wants us to be set apart and to man our post so that when the enemy sneaks around from the outside, we are ready and can tackle our opponent. We need the reminders just like the ten-year-old boys do. We so easily forget that we have a position to hold.

CHALLENGE: What activities tend to pull you in? What are ways you can be "set apart"?

$\mathcal{D}ay$ 4

Earning my Superwoman cape

VERSE: Isaiah 26:4: "Trust in The Lord forever, for The Lord, The Lord, is the Rock eternal."

I was a chaperone on a field trip to a large amusement park. In the midway, a voice called out, "Let me guess your age within 2 years and you can win a prize….everyone is a winner!" I could not resist. After all, this was a month before I turned the big 4-0 and I wanted to know if I still had that youthful look. Much to my chagrin, she guessed I was 45. FORTY-FIVE!!??!?! Oh well, I still won the pink sequined cape.

Throughout my life, I have had many insecurities. Many times, I felt I just did not measure up. There are some legitimate reasons I have felt this way and some irrational fears. Nonetheless there have been days that insecurities brought me deep in the valley. Some are silly insecurities for which I compensate – like wearing heels because I am short or reloading my deodorant JUST to make sure. Some insecurities have prompted constructive habits – like having a strong work ethic and to exercise on a fairly consistent basis. Some of my insecurities are deep-rooted and crop up in strange places.

Over the years, I have learned a few lessons. First, my security must rest with God and not with random circumstances. I am a child of the King who provides a security that cannot be matched on any human level. Second, I have learned that we all have some type of insecurities. Insecurities range from appearances, money, the house we live in, the job we ascribe to, our cooking ability, our intelligence level, and so on.

Once I realized that we are all in this together and that we all have our battles to face, my insecurities began to wither.

I can truly say that I am more secure in who I am – and more importantly WHOSE I am – than ever before. I still have nay-sayers, people who seem to know the exact place where my insecurities lie but it does not rock my world anymore. I may not be confident in myself some days, but I am confident in the ONE who made me!

I will wear my "Super Stockman" cape and proudly proclaim that I am tickled pink that God has brought me this far! I am thankful I have learned to find security in something besides circumstances or problems I have created in my mind. I stand on the Rock!

CHALLENGE: What are your insecurities....those areas that trip you up? Is there something in your behavior you need to change? Or do you need to remember where true security resides???

Day 5

I hate my job!

VERSE: John 4:35b: "I tell you, open your eyes and look at the fields! They are ripe for harvest."

Sometimes I hate my job. The paperwork is too much. I hate that there are politicians who have never talked to me that make big decisions about what I do. I put in way too many hours and miss important family time. I shiver to think of the amount of money I have spent buying wrapping paper, cookie dough, cases of drinks, candles, chicken biscuits, candy for my office, school supplies for students who do not have any, postage, and so on. I am sure I could buy myself a nice vacation with all that money! There is never a moment of peace or solitude in my office as there are always four happenings going on at once. All of that is fine!

The reason I hate my job sometimes is when my colleagues and I cannot get through to some students and they take the wrong path over and over. I hate that they sometimes do not have people in their life who CARE about them and they feel the only path is to drop out. I hate when they do not see the value of education and how it can take them to new places. I hate when grown-ups act like school is "against" the students because it is really "for" them. I hate that they do not realize when we teach discipline, it really has little to do with the here and now, but for developing skills for the future. I hate there are 100 awesome occurrences that happen every day, but if one BAD thing happens that is all anyone wants to talk about. People get the wrong impression and do not realize how AWESOME our kids are. I hate that people do not realize that, for most teachers, this is a mission, a PASSION – and that it is never about a paycheck. We invest our money – and our heart and soul into these students. We take them home in our spirits. Our spouses know about our students – how we worry about them, how we want them to be safe and happy and successful. We pray for them and cry over them when they hurt.

Until I stop hating those things, I will press on. We will band together and fight through doing more with less, finding a balance between work and home, and trying to spot that nugget of potential in a kid who seems not to care. We will fight for our future.

If only I had that same passion for people who do not know Jesus!!!!

CHALLENGE: Ask yourself what your passion is. Truly - what is it?? We all have preoccupations we hold near and dear to our hearts. Now find a way to help others!

$\mathcal{D}ay$ 6

My little red wagon

VERSE: Philippians 1:6: "Being confident of this, that he who began a good work in you will carry it on to completion until the day of Christ Jesus."

Nine years ago, this wagon was shiny red without a blemish. It had strong wooden sides and a huge, colorful bow on the handle. It was a gift from the grandparents for my twin boys' first birthday. Wow, did we use that wagon! I pulled them a million miles in that wagon. I loved how the wooden sides to keep them contained. It was such a convenient way to pull them with their toys and a snack. I pulled them to the pool and to take cookies to military families who moved in our neighborhood. I pulled them at the Fall Festival to see all the animals and the pumpkins. I pulled them to the baseball park to watch our nephew hit a couple home runs. Ruby, our babysitter, pulled them in the wagon every day to visit friends in the cul-de-sac. If you look through our photo albums, you will see that little red wagon in many venues.

Over the years, the little red wagon has lost much of her glamor. Last week, I was using the wagon – with no wooden sides, with lots of rust spots and tons of blemishes – to haul sticks to the ditch. Then I used it as I weeded around the blueberry bushes.

I realized I am a lot like that little red wagon. I am getting older with a few blemishes. I am not as shiny as I once was and my skin sags a little and I am not as skinny as I once was and I even needed a chemical peel to remove some age spots from my forehead. Even though my appearance may be different, I am still useful. My tasks may have changed over the years and probably will again. God is not finished using the little red wagon and He is not quite ready to put me beside the curb.

Just because I cannot do what I once could for the Kingdom does not mean that I cannot do something. I am excited to know that God is not finished with me – just like I am not finished with my little red wagon.

CHALLENGE: Instead of moaning about what you CANNOT do, decide something you CAN do? Now, go DO something!

Day 7

LIVE!

VERSE: John 10:10b: "I have come that they may life, and have it to the full."

He came that we might have LIFE and have it ABUNDANTLY! Living means constantly growing and reaching new heights in our relationship with Him. When we start to wither, we are not living, we are dying. I was reminded about overflowing abundance more than I imagined.

The year I turned forty was declared the "Year of Adventure" and celebrated by engaging in some type of adventure each month during the year. One Saturday was set aside for the July adventure. A friend and I went for a skydive while my guys were all on a Boy Scouts campout. We went and had a great time! It was breathtaking and fun and the pictures are incredible. This is not where I learned about abundance.

I must admit, I sighed a little when I got the phone call. I enjoyed having the bed – and the remote – all to myself. But, they called and asked me to join them the last night of the campout. So, I threw a change of clothes and a toothbrush in a bag and hopped in the jeep. I am SO incredibly glad I did. I got to see my guys doing all kinds of fun events – dress up like a real knight, play watermelon football, shoot a bow and arrow and a BB gun, get ready for a rocket launch, laugh with their friends, hug their dad during the worship service, and run to give me the biggest squeeze because I had not seen them in a couple days. What could possibly be more ABUNDANT than that? I get so wrapped up in thinking that abundance means having some great adventure, when abundance is truly found in the simple – the people in our path, our daily blessings, in the small ways life touches my heart.

When I get stressed with the troubles of this world, when work has me all "worked up", when I get frustrated because of the dishes in the sink, I have to stop and remember what an ABUNDANT life really is! I have Jesus in my heart, a husband by my side and kiddos at my feet. Not to mention so many other blessings! Today I will focus on the abundance God has given me, not the factors that take my eyes off of LIVING!

CHALLENGE: No matter our circumstances, He has called us to live abundantly! That doesn't mean having an abundance of THINGS, but having an abundance of HIM! What is robbing your joy? Ask yourself and be honest in your answer.

Day 8

Yes, I guess I need some help

VERSE: Proverbs 18:24: "A man of many companions may come to ruin, but there is a friend who sticks closer than a brother."

This morning I was in a twit! It began with the relentless conversation of "HURRY UP! We have to get ready and go!" I do not understand why a ten-year-old cannot follow the same routine we have engaged in for the past 6 years nor can I understand the need for a 15-minute shower in the morning while trying to get everything together and everyone out the door nor can I understand why some days just do not seem to "work". Today was one of those days!

Before I could even get to work, I received several "I have a problem" phone calls. The red light was on my phone in the office, meaning someone had called since the evening before, no doubt to complain. There was a stack of work on my desk that from the day before, and the alarm was going off at the end of the hall.

I was defeated. There was not any ONE thing wrong, it just was ALL wrong. I wanted to go home and get back in bed. What was the point of this every day? I was tired, my feet hurt already, and I forgot my earrings. I glanced at a plaque in my office with a Bible verse. At that very moment I knew I had a choice. I truly was defeated. I could stay in that dark place or I could climb out of the mental hole. I almost did not want to as I was plenty content to tell everyone how tired I was and that these complaining people drive me nuts. Something inside spoke loudly and clearly…..go pray! Pray – but I am already at work. "Go and pray!"

So, I found a friend of faith. She has known me for a very long time. I am the big sister in our relationship, so it was almost hard. I found myself saying out loud, "I need you to pray. I simply do not have the words today." We found a corner and she grabbed my hands and she prayed.

My soul smiled. I walked back to my office. The light was still red, the stack was still there, and my feet still hurt. However, I sure had a different perspective. Next time I hear that voice, I will not be reluctant to follow. Asking for help made ALL the difference!

CHALLENGE: When you are at the end of your rope – do not be afraid to ask someone to lift you up! In the same way, when you see a friend who seems defeated, be bold. Go pray with her. It will lift you both up!

Day 9

Cleaning up for the Housekeeper

VERSE: Jeremiah 33:3: "Call to me and I will answer you and tell you great and unsearchable things you do not know."

Once a month, I treat myself to a housekeeper. It eases my mind. She does the basics - dusts, vacuums, mops, washes the rugs, and so on. I love the smell that hits my nose the second I open the door after she has visited. It is good to come home to a freshly cleaned house after a long day of work. I am calm and relaxed!

The night before is a totally different story. I go into crazy-mom mode. Everyone has to clean up their school papers. We go through the stack of mail on the bar and make sure everyone puts up their shoes that are scattered about the house. After all, the housekeeper is coming and we have GOT to get this house cleaned up! I want her to think we live perfect, tidy lives during the other 29 days of the month. It would be a travesty to recognize that there is an occasional dish left in the sink or a towel on the floor. I make sure everyone makes their bed and that everything gives the appearance of being perfect. I drop in bed, exhausted, after cleaning up so the housekeeper can come the next morning.

Sometimes, my relationship with God is like that. Before I will go to Him in prayer, I try to get my act together. It would be a travesty for Him to realize that I am not perfect - that sometimes I leave my pride in the way or that I neglect to follow through with good intentions or that I do not manage my mouth as I should. I gather together all the Sunday School words I know and I pray.

The funny thing is that neither of these relationships are real. If the truth were told, my housekeeper knows that I picked up for her benefit. It is not as if she is unaware that I sincerely need her help. However, I try to cover up the blemishes. God knows us better and more intimately than any housekeeper. When I come to Him with my polished words and phrases for His benefit, He is unimpressed. After all, He knows I need Him! He knows every thought and every blemish underneath those words. How much more incredible would our relationship be if I did not clean up before I came to Him, but was honest and totally real?

CHALLENGE: Be real in your prayers. God can handle it! He already knows what is in your heart, so share it with Him - even if it hurts! It is amazing how that deepens your relationship in ways you could never imagine!

Day 10

Swimming pools

VERSE: Zephaniah 3:17: "The Lord your God is with you, He is mighty to save. He will take great delight in you, he will quiet you with his love, he will rejoice over you with singing."

As I sat in an airplane one afternoon I started praying. It was one of those days I wanted to hear a special word from God. As we began our descent into the airport, I opened the cover for my window and peered at the ground below. I was thinking God would speak to me about my place in the world and how we are part of a bigger picture and I needed to have a broader perspective. That is not at all where God took me.

What I could not stop noticing were the swimming pools. Those were the houses that caught my attention. That bright blue just popped!!! It was not the biggest houses or the worst houses....just the ones with the swimming pools. Something about that little "extra" glimmer from way up high set those houses apart. Even when I tried to focus on something else, I could not help noticing the shimmer from the swimming pools. They were like a magnet!

What could I learn from a swimming pool from thousands of feet in the air??? Christianity is like a swimming pool!! It washed over me to a place of understanding. We are all vessels but what sets us apart is Christ in us. It is the something "extra" that draws people to catch their eye. No matter what our outside looks like, when we have a shimmering pool, others take notice for a closer look. The difference He makes in us draws people in like a magnet. They want to know what makes the difference.

Even when those around us do not realize they are looking for something different and even we do not know the questions to ask, we are all built with a desire to know Him and are drawn to those whose light shines through. After all it is never about what I can say or do, but what He does through me. Just like it was not the house that caught my attention, but the pool that set it apart.

I just was not expecting to learn about Him through seeing a swimming pool from an airplane.

CHALLENGE: Take a look at your life. What sets you apart? Do you have that something "extra" that draws others to you? That something "extra" is Christ in you.

Day 11

Happy right where I am

VERSE: Philippines 4:11: "I am not saying this because I am in need, for I have learned to be content whatever the circumstances."

A friend and I met for a girl trip in a large city. While I was there, we met up with a friend that I had not seen since college. We had a great time at an Italian restaurant for hours catching up on our lives now, how our families are doing, and re-living memories of college days. It was such a great visit. It was a little bit of worlds colliding for me since I knew these two from very different phases of my life. However, it was fun to share stories, laugh together and give each a glimpse into different phases of our paths. After all I am still the same person, just with a few more wrinkles.

We have all taken different journeys and we talked about how God has brought us through various trials and situations - some very painful. We talked about being angry with God, but then later realizing it was all for our good. It was awesome to share that we all had a common thread that we were happy right where we are. We have very different paths, and there was a moment I felt insignificant as I have not traveled the world nor do I fly first class. Only for a moment though. Because we have all suffered great loss and received incredible blessings. We are children of the same King.

I am the one in the group that spends more time at a ballpark than an airport. One friend has taken photographs of some of the most beautiful people in North America. One friend has shattered sales goals all over her territory. At the end of the day we all shared that we are HAPPY. That happiness is a choice - it comes from a joy deeply rooted in knowing that God is in control. We all shared times we have struggled and been brought to the lowest valley. It is simply amazing how we can find happiness right in the middle of whatever circumstance God has us in whenever we choose to do so.

Why? Because whatever that circumstance is at the moment has absolutely no bearing on the fact that my future is secure in Him. As I look at the knots of everyday life from the bottom of my tapestry, I am excited to know that a beautiful picture of my life is being woven at that very moment.

CHALLENGE: Stop the pity party! We ALL have a story. We all have struggles. Look for happiness in the eternal, not in the temporary.

Day 12

Make a STOP doing list

VERSE: Romans 12:4-5: "Just as each of us has one body with many members, and these members do not all have the same function, so in Christ we who are many for one body, and each member belongs to all the others."

Several years ago, I was in charge of a Curriculum Retreat for a group of elementary teachers and leaders. We spent two days a 4-H center tucked away in central Alabama. We tackled many issues we were facing in our schools and we tackled teamwork activities on a low ropes course and a zip line. It was a time of intense work and intense fun. We had many hard decisions to make and worked to build a better program for our district. During one session, I put up a dry erase board and wrote the following words: ACTIVITIES WE WILL STOP! We had spent much time putting some plans in place to roll out to the schools in a few weeks. We were adding some strategies that required additional work but that would be extremely beneficial.

I have lived long enough to know that there are only so many minutes in an hour, so many hours in a day. To ADD something, we must STOP something. This was a particularly tough session because there were many sacred cows - activities we did not want to give up. We debated, we threw out ideas, we trashed a couple, we kept some, we wrote some actions in pencil because we were not quite sure, and we even argued a little. In the end we traded some GOOD actions for some GREAT undertakings.

Truthfully we had to do the same thing the next year. Even a couple matters we thought were great last year had to be reassessed. My Christian walk is like that. Sometimes I engage in activities simply because someone asked me to. It might not be that it is related to my spiritual gifts or even what I feel led to be involved in. Someone asks me to do something else, and I feel guilted into saying "yes". I need to hit the pause button and assess what I have put on my plate. I do not have to do EVERYTHING. That is a sure way to burn out the flame intended to light up the world.

What activities occupy your time? Are they GOOD? Are they GREAT? What sacred cows are you holding onto that you need to relinquish? Write them down - on paper - and see what needs to stay and what needs to go.

CHALLENGE: Share your STOP doing list with a trusted friend. Pray over it. Be honest and make the hard decisions.

Day 13

Sometimes you just have to ask

VERSE: James 3:5: "Likewise the tongue is a small part of the body, but it makes great boasts. Consider what a great forest is set on fire by a small spark."

In my line of work, I often hear rumors. Students tend to talk about someone with a nugget of truth and a whole lot of embellishment. More times than I would like to recount, a girl comes to me very upset about something that has been posted on social media or that someone is making fun of her for one reason or another. I then have to call in the other student and we talk about it. Usually, that resolves the situation. It is amazing how opening the lines of communication frequently help the situation.

This is not only true of children, but of adults. It seems that we all like to embellish a good story sometimes to sensationalize something with a nugget of truth. We see it in magazines at the supermarket checkout counter. And, we see it in our personal lives. I guess I thought people grew out of starting rumors. I have a friend rumored to be in a specific line of business across the country. When the news got back to me, it was as if this friend was in a seedy business. I was surprised, but, over time, I assumed it was truth. Much time went by and I actually had the opportunity to see this friend. To be honest, I was a little nervous. I wondered if we still had the basic principles of our character in common anymore.

So, we visited and chatted. Then, I swallowed hard, took a deep breath, and took my own advice. I just asked her. She was flabbergasted to say the least. A conversation ensued that assured me that I had heard rumors. At almost 40 years old rumors still hurt and they were still false. In a matter of minutes, I was able to put aside the wonderings I'd had for years. It was also an opportunity to figure out where the rumors started and how to correct them. A relationship was restored. We were able to have a great visit and share stories of the journey God has had us travel. I heard how she continues to minister in her business and in her personal life. It was amazing!

We do not always know the truth about a person's heart. We make lots of assumptions and believe all the hoopla is accurate. This encounter also reminded me not to spread "prayer requests" with the wrong motives. Seeing the hurt on my friend's face was enough to remind me to always go to the source.

CHALLENGE: Do not believe everything you hear. Sometimes, God will prompt your heart to go and ask. Spreading rumors is prevalent today – do not participate on either side!

Day 14

I'll pray for you. Let me know if you need anything.

VERSE: 2 Thessalonians 1:11: "With this in mind, we constantly pray for you, that our God may count you worthy of his calling, and that by his power he may fulfill every good purpose of yours and ever act prompted by your faith."

I am the world's worst friend sometimes. I never know the right thing to say and I am not the one who brings the right gift. I have the best intentions in the world, but I fail to follow through on many occasions. I was that person who always signed a card, "let me know if you need anything" and "I will pray for you". I often beat myself up because I sincerely want to be a good friend.

People (myself included) have often said that it is not the "right" words or the "right" gift that makes a difference. It is the fact we are there that makes a difference. In the same way, I was challenged several years ago about saying "I will pray for you". I really meant it at the time. Then life happened and I often forgot to pray. I tried to write items down and have even occasionally set my phone to vibrate at specific times of the day to remind me to pray for specific people/situations. After a particularly incredible and challenging Sunday School lesson, I stopped saying (not totally, but close) that I would pray for people. I would ask - right then and there - if I could pray with them. This has produced some of the most fantastic moments of my life. I have had precious moments in my office, in the parking lot of Walmart, in downtown Atlanta, in the hospital, and other various places. We have shed tears of joy and of sadness, celebrated miraculous healing, and felt complete devastation of a life lost. Every single time we have felt God's presence and peace.

I am proud to say that one of the most awesome decisions of my Christian walk is when I stopped saying I would pray for people, and actually started praying! I am thankful for a Sunday School teacher who speaks truth and challenges my walk! I am thankful for a God who is steadfast and faithful. I am thankful for those with whom I have prayed and count is as an honor to speak the name of family, friends and strangers before the throne.

This is dedicated to "Aunt Reba" who taught me that prayer is a powerful blessing!

CHALLENGE: Find someone today who needs prayer. Invite them to lunch and pray over them. Call them and pray over them - out loud. It may feel awkward, but you both will receive an incredible blessing.

Day 15

The Marble Horse

VERSE: Isaiah 41:10: "So do not fear, for I am with you; do not be dismayed, for I am your God. I will strengthen you and help you; I will uphold you with my righteous right hand."

I am pretty much a marble slab.

There exists a story in legend that a famous sculptor, who had shaped a gorgeous horse out of marble, was asked how he could create a horse out of a slab. He caused pause when he said that he simply looked at the slab of marble and saw a horse. Then he chiseled away anything that did not look like the horse.

Our spiritual lives mimic that mental image. When we see ourselves, we often see a slab of marble. We hope and wish we could be a work of art. However, we need a master craftsman. That is where God comes in. He does not see a slab of marble, but rather an intricate, beautifully designed horse (figuratively, of course). He then begins to chisel away every piece of marble (every piece of me) that does not look like the work of art (Him).

Sometimes, he chisels a big chunk of marble. Those represent big events in our lives that shaped us. Other times, He chisels minuscule pieces of marble to create a intricate design. Those are the moments we sometimes take for granted and sometimes overlook and sometimes over-react and sometimes act extremely frustrated. These are the times that provide the details of our lives that make us unique.

When some pieces fall off, it is often a struggle for us. Because that means we have to give something up. We have to let go. While it is sometimes easy to hold onto that piece of marble, we will never become a true work of art without His touch. So, do not be dismayed during times of large struggle or small frustrations. For it is in those times you are truly becoming a stunning creation by a master craftsman. When we are called to let go of some pieces (habits, how we use our tongue, guilt, and so on) and we have those moments we wonder if it is worth it to let go of our comfort to become a masterpiece, remember His promises! Celebrate the pieces that fall away as we know that shedding unnecessary details means looking more like The Creator a little more and who He intended us to be!

One of these days, I will be a beautiful marble masterpiece!

CHALLENGE: Celebrate the times when pieces fall off that do not look like Christ. He is chiseling you into a beautiful masterpiece. Take time to thank Him right now for loving you enough to chisel away!

Day 16

Limitless

VERSE: Psalm 147:5: "Great is our Lord and might in power; his understanding has no limit."

I am a fairly outgoing person. Those who know me would not hesitate to agree. However, many people do not know that I have to have some quiet and alone time to recharge my batteries. I need to spend a bit of time most days to simply chill out - read a book, watch a mindless movie, play a random card game. I do not fly often, but if I am flying by myself, this is the perfect time for me to unwind. I tend to pop in a piece of gum, put my headphones on and crank up the iPad to get lost in various activities. It is almost like I am in a world of my own. A few weeks ago, I found myself flying home from Dallas after five days being away from home. I'd had an awesome time, but was ready to see my family. After a long layover, I was ready to get lost in nothingness for the last couple hours before seeing my loves.

As I was putting my carry-on bag in the overhead compartment, I realized it was heavier coming back home than when I left (I had to get prizes for the guys) and found myself flexing my muscles a little. A gentleman quickly came to the rescue. In a matter of circumstance (or divine appointment), he was seated beside me. At first, I felt obligated to talk with him. He was from San Antonio and asked if I had ever been. I told him of the summer I spent as a college student summer missionary. He began to ask questions about my faith. I asked about his and encouraged him to find himself involved in some type of ministry.

I talked about it being such a blessing any time I helped others. He said he always tried to be a "light" in his job and hoped it would lead to conversations about The Lord. We chatted off and on for the next half hour or so. Then, I kind of dozed off.

When I awoke, he was reading a copied chapter of a Bible study. He was reading through and making notes. He shared with me that his wife had wanted him to do this study with her and that he was encouraged to go ahead and do it after our chat. He said that the study was about God being "limitless" and that He cares about every single aspect of our lives.

The man shook my hand as we de-planed and thanked me for encouraging him to remember that God IS limitless and that we really could not ask for anything more. He walked away thinking I had encouraged him. What he did not know is that I was the one encouraged. I serve a God who cares more about my character and a meeting of divine intervention far more than my comfort.

CHALLENGE: As you travel about to your job, to the grocery store or to a faraway city, be attuned to the fact that God has divine encounters meant to sow seeds of faith and to strengthen your own faith. Look for something miraculous to happen today from an ordinary circumstance.

Day 17

The Apples in a Seed

VERSE: Galatians 6:9: "Let us not become weary in doing good, for at the proper time we will reap a harvest if we do not give up."

Sometimes I get tired of being a Christian, of doing the "right" thing. Sometimes it seems like it does not even matter! There are days I want to throw caution to the wind, speak my mind completely, and forget Who I represent. Does anybody notice? Does anybody care?

Then I remember what my purpose is. My purpose is to plant seeds wherever I go. There is a saying that frequently rings in my spirit, "You can count the seeds in an apple, but you cannot count the apples in a seed." What profound wisdom. In my own strength, I can only see the fruit of my labor that is right in front of my face. If I spend my time trying to be "good" so that I see the fruit of my labor, then it is in vain. It reminds me of one of my boys at five years old. He wanted to plant an apple tree so he could eat apples over the summer. He was so disappointed we were not able to pick an apple nearly that quickly.

Planting seeds is about leaving a legacy. We will never know the impact we will have if we stay true to His word even on the hard days. In the 1980s, First Call sang a song with a poignant line, "All we have to offer is the legacy we leave behind". It seems to me that we, myself included, are often worried about how many seeds are in our apples - how many blessings we can gather. How our life stacks up with others and how we can have an apple with more seeds than everyone else.

If we were more focused on planting, we would have baskets overflowing with apples! At my house, we have planted a garden for many years and I am constantly amazed at the crop that grows because my husband works the soil and tends to the mundane. He goes out every morning. Every single morning. That is how I have to live my Christian life - every single day. That does not mean I will not MESS up, but it does mean that I will not GIVE up!

I will plant seeds. I will not give up. I will let God count the apples in my seeds!

CHALLENGE: Stop browbeating yourself for not being perfect. Focus on continuing the faith and on leaving a legacy. That is far more important than a one-shot moment of being awesome.

Day 18

How to pray and get what I want

VERSE: Psalm 37:4: "Delight yourself in The Lord, and He will give you the desires of your heart."

Ever since college, this has been one of my favorite life verses (do you have life verses? You should. It is amazing how God uses them at specific times in my life!). My blonde-headed friend bought me the most beautiful plaque with that verse that has made every single move with me. It is one of His greatest promises.

I loved this verse because I held onto the promise that as long as I sang a few praise songs and prayed every day and worked at Vacation Bible School, then God would bless with me with those fascinations that I really wanted!! Not the mundane objects, but I just knew He would give me what I really wanted. I always looked at that blue plaque with a smile in my heart and satisfaction in my soul.

Then, life happened. I did not always get the desires of my heart. I prayed for something specific for many years and God was silent. "But I am singing in a Christian group and I am leading a discipleship group and blah blah blah". This was a promise in His Word, right? I was so confused.

Until I read the verse again! See, my problem was that I was reading it backwards. I started with the desires of my heart and then snuck a little Jesus in my life and asked Him to bless my plans. That is not how it works. It starts with delighting myself in The Lord. When I do that, the desires of my heart change. They are no longer wrapped in my success or making sure events turn out like I want them to or have God's blessings on what I think is best for my life. The desires of my heart change when I TRULY delight myself in Him. Those desires are more about finding ways to minister to others and serving and praying for family and friends and how I can grow closer to Him and how I can have wisdom about His Word. When those become the desires of my heart, I get exactly what I pray for and nothing less.

Psalm 37:4 continues to be one of my favorite life verses, but for very different reasons than 20 years ago. I am thrilled to serve a God who wants to give me the desires of my heart as I delight in Him!

CHALLENGE: What makes you happy? Is it the eternal or temporary? If we focus our attention on the God of the eternal, it will be amazing that the desires of our heart remains full!

Day 19

The fundamentals of basketball

VERSE: Deuteronomy 6:5: "Love The Lord your God with all your heart and with all your soul and with all your strength."

For many years, I worked at a Christian Children's Camp. I loved it! I actually started as a camper when I was in the second grade. The Bible Lady came to our school and I completed monthly lessons so I could receive a partial scholarship to attend camp for a week in the summer. Through the years, I became a C.I.T. (Counselor in Training) in high school and a counselor while I was in college. I cannot begin to describe how much I grew spiritually and emotionally during that time. I learned scripture and dug deep into God's Word. I had friends who helped make incredible memories and who held me accountable.

During my high school years, I struggled to figure out the differences in some church practices and some core beliefs. See, the camp was inter-denominational. Since the people I worked with were from different churches, albeit all evangelical, I started asking some hard questions. Is it okay to have a piano in the church? Is baptism by emersion necessary? How often do I have to go to church? What does predestination mean? Can you lose your salvation?

During that time, I had a missionary friend who often challenged me pretty significantly. One evening, we had a lengthy and lively discussion about baptism. He asked me if I was going to be wrapped up in the rules or in winning people to Christ. WOW! As I lay in bed one particular night, God showed me a great mental picture to which I could relate.

Christian denominations are like a basketball team. Each group runs plays a little differently. Some run a man-to-man defense while others run a zone. Each team has special plays to accomplish the task of scoring points. However, there are fundamentals that are necessary for every basketball team. Running, passing, shooting, dribbling.....those are fundamentals. How you execute the fundamentals is what makes teams unique.

Christianity has fundamentals, too. The immaculate conception, His crucifixion, His ascension into heaven, the forgiveness of sins.... these are all fundamentals. However, there are small details that are simply the design of a basketball play. It was freeing to me to realize that so many of us were playing the same game with the same fundamentals of Christ. That made the details less important and the overall message shine through. It took my focus off legalistic details and placed them appropriately on advancing what really matters!

CHALLENGE: Are you focused on what truly matters? Sometimes we allow "hypocrites" to stand between us and God. If so, the hypocrite is standing closer. As I grow in my relationship with God, I am less concerned about minute details and more concerned about the salvation of others.

Day 20

Those little red boxes

VERSE: Galatians 1:10: "Am I now trying to win the approval of men, or of God? Or am I trying to please men? If I were still trying to please men, I would not be a servant of Christ."

It is amazing how fickle our self-esteem is. One minute we are flying high and the next minute we have shattered feelings.

During the month of November, the Facebook community often posts something to be thankful for each day. When you post something, people can comment on your post or they can "like" it. Usually, a few people stop in on my posts. I noticed for about a week that I did not have any little red boxes notifying me that someone "liked"what I had said. I found myself sad and questioning if people no longer valued what I had to say. About half way into a self-induced pity party, I realized I was being ridiculous. If I attached my worth to the number on the little red boxes of Facebook, I was completely unaware of Who holds my worth. God and I had a heart-to-heart. Actually, I felt chastised because I was completely seeking the approval of men, even though many of my posts were about Christ.

God's Word says that if we seek the approval of men that we reap our reward here on earth. If we are truly seeking the approval of Him, we will receive our reward in heaven. Even if I am a "do-gooder", it is all in vain if I do it with the wrong motives. So, I listened when He reminded me that my worth is in Him, in my salvation. He holds my future in His hands and He guides my steps. Every aspect of my life has passed through His fingertips. His promises are true, and He will never let me go. My goal should not be to please those around me, but to please the One who made me. If I lay my treasures in people thinking I am good, I will miss the true treasure of the One who calls me His own.

A couple days later, I realized a setting was wrong on my Facebook that locked all my posts - no one had even seen them. The lesson I learned from a random setting was worth far more than any number of "likes". It helped re-focus my motives from the temporary to the eternal.

CHALLENGE: Take an honest inventory of yourself. Do you measure the value of what you have to say by how many "likes" or "retweets" you receive? Do you constantly look to see how many followers you have? If you focus on your relationship with Christ instead of who approves of you, then you will find the best approval rating possible - that of the King!

Day 21

Be Still and Know

VERSE: Psalm 46:10: "Be still and Know that I am God; I will be exalted among the nations, I will be exalted in the earth."

Several years ago, I went through a particularly rough time in my vocation. My job, along with about ten others, were on the line due to budget cuts. There was also some ugliness associated with the job cuts. This particular group of people who hung in the balance were some of the most Godly people I know, and some of my closest friends. During this struggle, several of us talked. No matter how yucky the situation became, we were insistent that we walk through this time with our integrity in tact. After all, everyone knew we were believers. What better way to let our light shine? A wise lady talked to a couple in our group and said that sometimes God wants us to "be still". It was the very nature of everyone in this group to take action, but this became our verse.

There were some dark days - days that we individually and collectively wanted to give up. In God's divine wisdom, He always had at least one person to be strong at a time. We shared that verse frequently. We texted it, we e-mailed it, we wrote it on note cards and left it on each other's chairs. We prayed together and we prayed for each other. Over about eight months, this was our verse.

One by one, the members in our group secured their positions for the next year. There were two of us still waiting. Being still was becoming increasingly difficult. Didn't God need my help??? Then, my friend secured a spot. The day I was supposed to start a new contract, I was unsure where to show up for work. I called the boss to ask. He loosely gave me an option of two places and I chose one (which was quite obvious). The job was very much out of my comfort zone! He asked me to go meet the principal the next morning. So, I called and scheduled a meeting.

When I arrived, he met me at the front and we walked around the school and talked. I shared with him my experience and my strengths and weaknesses. He shared with me some needs of the school. We then walked to his office. I sat across from his desk. Behind the desk was a tall bookshelf. Right above his head was a glass etching that said, "BE STILL AND KNOW". I am certain he continued talking, but God and I were having a moment. At that very second, I knew He had prepared the perfect opportunity at the perfect time. I knew He had not forgotten me.

Integrity? I hope so. A life blessing? Without a doubt!!!

CHALLENGE: When areas of your life are dismal at the moment and you cannot understand what God is up to, know that sometimes He wants us to BE STILL and let Him show out. He has NOT forgotten you!!

Day 22

Hocus Focus

VERSE: Psalm 106: 1-2: "Praise The Lord. Give thanks to The Lord, for he is good; his love endures forever. Who can proclaim the might acts of The Lord?"

It seems like the moment I turned 40, life began to change. Some were good changes - I became more confident in who I am and I realized that life is too short to neglect DOING events I have only TALKED about. However, there are a couple issues that have not been so great. My metabolism is slowing down, my right knee creaks when I run and my eyesight is becoming 'hesitant'.

There are an increasing number of times it takes me a minute to focus on the words in front of me. My eyes adjust, but it takes a second and I have to concentrate a bit more than in times past. I hate when I look at a book and it is fuzzy; but, I love it when the words become clear. It happens when I focus - on purpose.

Being thankful requires focus! Sometimes life, at first glance, seems a little fuzzy and cloudy, even negative. However, when we - on purpose - count our blessings and express our thanks to God (and to people who make a difference in us), it is amazing how my whole perspective changes. Yes, we all go through tough times, and I am not thankful for some situations I have had to endure. But, any day that I wake up this side of the dirt is a true blessing. It means the good outweighs the bad. It means I still have a purpose to fulfill.

As you travel your personal journey, concentrate on being thankful. It will change your entire attitude and it will become contagious to those around you! Keep a journal, make a mental list, log them in the Notes on your iPhone....whatever it takes!

To focus on being thankful does not require a magic trick.....just a willing spirit!

CHALLENGE: Begin today to thank God for blessings - small and large - in your life. Say it out loud! Send a note to 3 people that have made an impact on you. Less than $2 changes your perspective and it encourages others!

Day 23

Packing up Baby Jesus

VERSE: Luke 2:7: "And she gave birth to her firstborn, a son. She wrapped him in cloths and placed him in a manger, because there was no room for them in the inn."

One of my favorite days of the year is right after Thanksgiving when it is time to decorate for Christmas. First, we have to make sure the house is clean. After all, we are decorating for the King. All the legos are picked up, furniture is moved for the tree, and there are fresh vacuum tracks across the carpet. Then, I rally the troops to lug all the boxes (and boxes and boxes) down from the attic. The first decoration displayed every year is my nativity set, given to me by my best friend. It fills the entire table in my foyer and I absolutely love it. We play Christmas music and swap the items on the mantle for garland and stockings. It is a festive time for several hours until all our favorite items are placed in their annual spot and the empty boxes are returned to the attic.

Then we enjoy the holidays. It is a blessed holiday season as we celebrate the birth of our Savior and the beginnings of Christianity that culminate in Easter Sunday. We talk often about the REAL reason for the season and attend special church services to celebrate. My heart and my pocketbook somehow automatically become more giving, and I greet everyone from the mailman to the supermarket clerk with an extra smile.

Two days after Christmas, I have the itch! All the red and green start to get on my nerves. The tree sheds and I am ready for my normal decor to return. Once again, I rally the troops and and lug the boxes back down the stairs and replace all the items and restore normalcy. Carefully, I replace each piece of the nativity set in the original boxes. The last piece I put in the styrofoam packaging is Mary holding baby Jesus.

As I haul the boxes back to the attic one last time (until next year), I wonder if I'm packing up baby Jesus in more ways than one. Will I still have a giving spirit in January? Will I still greet the clerk with an extra smile? Will I talk about the Bible as much with the boys in June? These are the evidence of my relationship with him - not just the "feel-good" of the season. No wonder many people wonder about us Christians - if I would be so fickle about celebrating the true reason for Christmas, have I truly grsped the magnitude of the ultimate gift of the Son?

This year, maybe I won't pack up baby Jesus.

CHALLENGE: Pick something that reminds you of your relationship with God in a highly visible place. Never lose sight of what is important the whole year long, not just during the Christmas season.

Day 24

Magnificent Hues

VERSE: Psalm 19:1 "The heavens declare the glory of God; the skies proclaim the work of his hands."

One of my favorite sights is a sunset. I love the beautiful mix of pinks and purples as the sun begins its descent over the horizon. Never once have I tired of seeing the magnificent hues next to the sun. My family always gets tickled at me because no matter where we are, I will comment on a beautiful sunset. One of my favorite places to watch the sunset is at the beach. I am perfectly content with the world to sit in my chair and watch the entire process as the colors touch the sky and touch a part of my soul.

Just last week, we took a Sunday afternoon drive to the lake. All of a sudden, we took a turn and there it was. The sky was breathtakingly gorgeous in an array of purple. It was funny because we were in the middle of a conversation when I stopped to comment on the beauty. One of the boys made a remark that caught me off guard. He said, "Mom, the sunset was there for a while - you just were not looking in the right place". I thought on his comment for quite some time. He was right, after all. I had been looking at parts of the sky that were not close to the sun. That part of the sky was gray with streaks of clouds.

Truthfully, my life is like that. When I am close to the SON, my life is more radiant. I have had times in my life people have stated they were encouraged to live a life closer to God and to seek Him. Those are the times when I am in the Word and seeking Him myself. Those are days my colors are radiant because of His light. There are also times when those encouraging voices are silent. That is because I am living in my own power and seeking my own desires. Those days my sky is gray with streaks of clouds. When we are not next to THE light, our colors are dim.

If we truly want to make a difference in the world and to be a light in the darkness, we must stay close to the source of that light - and that is in the SON. Just like our electronic devices will not function once the battery runs dry and we have to recharge them from the source of power, we must stay recharged to our source. Otherwise, we run down and lose our functionality.

Our purpose is to glorify Him. If that is true, He wants my hues to be magnificent. That can only happen when I am close to the Son and His light reflects off my life.

CHALLENGE: Take a moment to reflect on your life at this moment. Are you reflecting His light or are you in the drab gray sky? What steps do you need to take to be close to the Son?

Day 25

Code of Ethics

VERSE: Romans 12:9: "Love must be sincere. Hate what is evil; cling to what is good."

Last week I attended a professional workshop about Ethics. It was sincerely a great presentation regarding Ethics Laws, Ethics Codes, and the like. We discussed a variety of topics within the parameters of education. Several scenarios were provided encompassing real-life activities. It was quite a lively discussion at several points, and we all thoroughly enjoyed both the formal presentation and the informal dialogue.

However, there was one slide that caught my eye. It was in the middle of the Code of Ethics presentation, which the speaker was providing a chronology of how Ethics Codes have evolved. The slide said, "The Bible: The First Code of Ethics". I guess I have never really thought of the Bible in that context. However, consider the tenets of The Word. There are the Ten Commandments, the Golden Rule, the Beatitudes, the Fruit of the Spirit, the Old Law and the New Covenant. Inside the pages of the scriptures lies the most encompassing and complete Code of Ethics in existence. There are scenarios played out in the lives of the Heroes of the Faith, in the parables of Jesus, and the lessons we learned in children's Sunday School.

By definition, "ethics" contain a system of moral principles or the rules of conduct recognized in respect to a particular group, culture, etc." Ethics reflect who we are and how what we do should impact people. It is concerning to me that our society is in a position of deciding if we should maintain ethics laws and how they should change so that we do not offend anyone by being rigid or too intrusive.

The truth is that we would not need ethics laws if we followed those outlined in the Bible. If we would learn to "Love God and Love People", we would not face the crises we do today. Of course, everyone does not read the Bible and we need guidelines and ethics laws. Believers who study the Bible already have a blueprint laid out for us to follow. God calls us to implement His Code of Ethics.

CHALLENGE: Do you tend to separate your spiritual life from the rest of your life? I have never considered the Bible as being the first Code of Ethics. Knowing this should help us focus on incorporating the very words of the scripture into the marrow of our being.

Day 26

Cherished Chit-Chat

VERSE: Deuteronomy 8:11: "Be careful that you do not forget The Lord your God, failing to observe his commands, his laws and his decrees that I am giving you this day."

A friend and I had children taking gymnastics at the same time. We were excited because every Wednesday afternoon, we had a walking date. We threw on our tennis shoes and wore out the track at the YMCA. I am certain we burned a few calories walking, but millions more by talking. We worked at the same school, had children around the same ages and husbands with similar personalities. While making our rounds on the track, we solved most of the world's problems.

One of the matters we discussed regularly was a struggle for both of us - neglecting our families too much because of work. We were both driven and wanted to make a huge impact on the students with whom we worked. In the meantime, our families were often in the crossfire of losing quality family time. Through our time walking, we worked to hold each other accountable. One of the greatest bonds God instituted was that of the family. We knew that if we did not work to keep our families strong, all other efforts would be in vain.

After this went on for about two years, she gave me the best Christmas present ever! It was in a beautifully wrapped box with a gorgeous bow. The note attached was simple, "We have enjoyed this...I hope you will, too". I was curious. After all, this was not Dirty Santa or a White Elephant Christmas exchange. When I opened it I had no idea the impact it would make! It was a jar with vinyl letters that said, "Cherished Chit-Chat" and was full of folded strips of paper with random questions. They ranged from "What was your favorite children's book?" to "Would you rather be the smartest or the most popular?" to hundreds in between. Every night at dinner, someone draws out a question. I had no idea how much fun we would have with this simple activity. Much conversation has been spurred, many laughs have been chuckled and we now have an insight to how our children think on a very intimate level. It is not that we did not talk to our boys - we do all the time. Somehow this was different. It is purposeful and generates open dialogue around the dinner table where everyone has a voice.

We often think that providing for our children is monetary - and part of it is. However, our obligation is deeper than sports and activities, trips and vacations, school supplies and homework....it is TIME! Time is the costliest and most critical gift we can provide.

CHALLENGE: Take inventory of whether you are spending time doing activities FOR your children or WITH them. Find simple ways (like Cherished Chit-Chat) to spend quality time that will pay far more dividends than their college fund!

Day 27

You don't trust me!

VERSE: Proverbs 3:5-6: "Trust in The Lord with all your heart, and lean not on your own understanding; in all your ways acknowledge him, and he will make your paths straight."

A couple nights ago, we went to some friends' house for dinner with several families. These are people we are very close to and are very comfortable with. The dads seem to migrate toward the den with the big-screen TV to watch a football game while the moms seem to find themselves around the dining room table munching on holiday cookies and chatting about the involvements of our children. We told funny stories and talked about how it is scary watching them grow up. Several moms have teenage daughters and they shared how tough it is to maintain standards in our current society. As they discussed curfews and the process of letting go, it became evident that the girls wanted their independence and tried to convince their moms that they would make good choices. When confronted with a midnight curfew instead of 2 am or told they could not a certain place, the girls often said, "You don't trust me!"

The truth is, I remember saying that to my mom as an all-knowing seventeen year old. I knew that statement bothered her. Now as I see teenagers in the halls of a high school, I hear some of those same conversations among friends.

As a mom and a grown-up, I have realized that my mom did not trust me completely, nor should she. She saw life from a different perspective and knew there were temptations and situations out there of which I was completely unaware.

Are we not like that with God? We ask Him to bless the plans we have made and get upset when He doesn't give in to our every whim. We do not understand why we cannot buy a certain house, get a specific job, or reach a particular weight. Just like a parent, He sees life from a different perspective. When our spirit screams out that "He just does not trust me", there is some truth in that sentiment. And, rightfully so! He knows traps ahead and temptations of which we are completely unaware. Those are the very reasons we have boundaries and guidelines in the Bible - to keep us safe.

So, the next time I start to whine like a teenage girl, I will remember that God is my Father and He is only looking out for my best interest.

CHALLENGE: Take an inventory of your prayer list. What items are you asking God to bless that may sound more like a whining teenage girl asking for a later curfew? Once you identify those areas, scratch them off your list.

Day 28

The Good Ole' Days

VERSE: Isaiah 43:18: "Forget the former things; do not dwell on the past."

The other day a group of friends gathered at a local Mexican restaurant that is the favorite of the guest of honor. Our special friend, Jan, retired the week before from a great career of 25 years in education. We all knew and loved her very much! And, our group always had a blast together. When one of our friends came in a little late, she even stated she was not looking for us, but listening for us. We laughed and began to recall memories over the past couple decades. We talked about crazy Christmas decorations, a zip line adventure, banana hair clips, random workshops, team-building games, folders of paperwork and stories about co-workers and children with whom we had all worked. We recalled stories of laughter, sadness over losses, and days of down-right insanity! We took pictures in all kinds of groups to memorialize another precious moment we were thankful our co-workers were truly friends.

During one tirade of stories, a friend next to me leaned over and said, "Those were the good ole' days, we just didn't know it". We did have several years a core group of folks worked closely together and believed in a "work hard, laugh hard" philosophy. Those WERE good days!

Truthfully, though, most days are GOOD days! We have so much to be thankful for every day - from our families (even the crazy parts), our jobs (or lack of a job which provides us time to give to others) to our health (or those whose lives we can touch while we are sick)! In ten years, I will remember today as "the good ole days". Why can't I love the moment NOW? Why is that we have to look back at our scrapbooks and photo albums to remember the good times? We are living the good times! God has truly blessed us and wants us to find the abundant life NOW - not always in hindsight. Maybe it is because we spend so much time looking for the next big adventure or something more fulfilling that we miss the RIGHT NOW that is so fulfilling!

So, here's to days of board games and cookie dough, of crazy schedules that include late nights at the ball park, of making memories with the people we work with every day, of dirty dishes and endless amounts of laundry, of the never-ending yard work and savings accounts that are lacking, of stay-cations rather than vacations, of buying from the sales rack, of pajama days and crying-filled nights. These ARE the good ole days.....the days we will remember in a few years that made our lives rich and full and complete. I will not wait until the next retirement - I will love today for today!

CHALLENGE: Look through an old photo album and write down 10 incidents that made you smile. Now, sit down and make a list of 10 reasons you smiled this week. Relish those moments and know that God gives you those moments because He loves you - endlessly loves you!

Day 29

Why NOT me???

VERSE: Isaiah 43:2-3a: "When you pass through the waters, I will be with you; and when you pass through the rivers, they will not sweep over you. When you walk through the fire, you will not be burned; the flames will not set you ablaze. For I am the Lord, your God, the Holy One of Israel, your Savior."

In my next book (insert smile here), I plan to write about "What a Difference a Day Makes" since we have all had days of total elation and those that brought us to our knees. I have started the research for the compilation of stories, and have a few "days" to add myself. Without going into detail, suffice it to say that I have a close friend who went through an extraordinarily BAD day! She survived an event no one should have to endure. To this day, on the anniversary date of this horrific event, she receives cards, calls and texts. Perhaps you have an event that reduced you to a puddle of tears or made you lose faith.

The incredible part about this story is her reaction. While I did not know her when her darkest day hit her square in the face, it was fresh the day she told me her story. We were sitting in a hotel chatting about the workshops we attended for the day. As dinner came and went, we began sharing our stories. She told me about her day and I listened with soggy eyes. She told how her friends gathered around for prayer and support. Then, she said something I will never forget that has changed me forever. When someone mentioned how unfair the situation was, my friend responded with, "What makes me think I am so special that

I can't have something bad happen to me? I am no better or worse than all God's children."

WOW! What words of wisdom! Sometimes we think that, because we go through a trial, God has forgotten us or we lose faith in the One who created us. We get angry at God for plopping us in the middle of heartache. Why do we encourage others who are in the middle of a crisis, but turn our backs when WE are the ones in that predicament? It must mean we think we are more special than everyone else. Ouch! Maybe that hits a little too close to home. We live in a fallen world where sin exists. As long as we are on earth, we will have troubles. We WILL. We are not so special to live our lives untouched while others take our fair share of troubles.

The next time I find myself with a problem on my hands or in the middle of a horrific day, I will not ask, "Why ME?" but rather I will say, "Why NOT me?" I will stand fast and hold true to the promises in the Word.

CHALLENGE: Think about the struggles you face. Recognize they are REAL and they often HURT. Then remember that God is not picking on you! We all face heartaches and times of uncertainty. Find yourself in a place of recognizing that you are not so special that you will not be spared those tough days.

Day 30

Lessons I learned from Lego's

VERSE: Proverbs 17:6: "Children's children are a crown to the aged, and parents are the pride of their children."

What in the world are little plastic blocks doing in the middle of a devotion book? Since I have boys that love them and they are constantly everywhere - all over the floor in the den, in the playroom, in their bedrooms, in my car, and the list goes on - I wanted to share them with you. I decided one week we were going to organize this mess! Of course, I was the only one in the house who cared for such a task. We had some frustration over what kind of system would be best - how they could see the blocks and how to keep them organized. We (I) spent a couple hours sorting by size. Then they informed me they wanted them organized by color. Insert SIGH here!!!!!! After some discussion and a shopping trip that ended at a Mexican restaurant to let everybody chill out, we came home with a plan. We spent some quality time sorting and sorting. An accident happened and I learned a couple lessons along the way.

1. The right pieces create a great product. Just like lego kits come with the right pieces to make a specific figure, God has a perfect plan for us. He gives us the exact pieces we need to make His plan work. Even though my boys love to get the kit based on the pictures on the front, they do not always put the kit together. When they do not, those pieces never quite live up to what they were made for.

2. Directions are included. I do not know why I keep all the books from the kits they have gotten - but I do. Because we cannot make the batmobile again without the directions, I guess. The direction books are designed to walk us through the process and give guidance along the way. Funny how we have a guidebook too!!!!

3. It takes all kinds of pieces to make a cool creation. The same is true in life. It takes all kinds of people - not just ones like me. It takes big bold pieces, tiny pieces that give the finishing touch and connecting pieces that no one ever sees. It would be boring only to have 6-peg red pieces!

4. Pieces left all over the floor are not serving their purpose. Sometimes we put ourselves in lonely places and sometimes we disconnect from others - emotionally if not physically. When we do not work with others, we never reach our full potential. We really do need each other.

5. I know my tubs will never last - there are already pieces on the floor. But, I also love watching them take the mixed-up pieces and create something lovely. It gives me hope for our lives. See, most of us do not stick the plan given on the cover of the box - the "perfect plan" for those pieces. I am so glad I serve a God who can take up the mixed-up pieces of my life and create something extraordinary out of it. That is pretty awesome!!!!!

As I near the end of sorting and picking up legos from all over the house, I am keenly aware that they will not stay this way just like I am keenly aware that I will not always put these lessons into practice. However, I know a few more strips of my tapestry are being woven into the fabric of my life. With each stitch, I am becoming more like the picture my master has for me.

CHALLENGE: Keep playing. Keep building. Keep learning.

Day 31

Naked Trees

VERSE: Jeremiah 17:8: "He will be like a tree planted by the water that sends out its roots by the stream. It does not fear when heat comes; its leaves are always green. It has no worries in a year of drought and never fails to bear fruit."

I love trees, especially in the winter. Do not get me wrong - I love to see spring buds as the earth comes to life when the weather warms up. But, I LOVE NAKED TREES - trees that have lost their leaves and stand with no covering as they continue to reach for the sky. Nothing hides her imperfections or the nests that have been built in the forks of her limbs. The winter sky is usually gray and provides a contrast to those branches stretching high. It is like they are not afraid to be who they really are.

As we drove to my see our family on Christmas Day, we passed a pecan orchard. We have passed it a thousand times. Yet, it caught my eye. As I pondered my affinity for naked trees, I wonder if the reason is because I am a little jealous. I work so hard at covering up my imperfections and hiding nests that consume my thoughts that I cannot be totally REAL. I sometimes pray no one sees the inside where my thoughts and motives live. We often try to wear the right covering - or mask - for whatever situation is at and. We are scared people will not love us for who we REALLY are. So, we cover our true selves with leaves of hobbies we do not like, procedures to make us more attractive, material possessions we do not even want, clothes that are in vogue, even participate in religious activities with the wrong motives, and the list goes on and on. Our insecurities often rob us of the joy of being exactly who we were created to be.

I wonder what would happen if we were stripped of our coverings and were totally REAL with each other. I wonder if we would learn that, while we are all unique, we are far more alike that we would like to admit. Shedding our leaves and showing our real selves can be scary, and it can be salve to the soul. Once we admit we are not perfect or that we are beautiful JUST as He created us to be, we realize that we have spent a lot of time in vain! God loves us for our stripped down, no leaves attached, selves. He sees us as we TRULY are, not as who we pretend to be.

Maybe we could learn a little from naked trees!

CHALLENGE: Get by yourself and ask some hard questions. Are you pretending to be someone you aren't? Do you know who you REALLY even are? Be honest with yourself and dig deep to find yourself unafraid to be who you were made to be.

$\mathscr{D\!AY}$ 32

Firm foundation

VERSE: 2 Timothy 2:19a: "Nevertheless, God's solid foundation stands firm, sealed with this inscription: 'The Lord knows who are his'."

It isn't about slaying dragons, but about building systems. It isn't about being a hero, but leaving a legacy.

I spoke these words to a group of educators who are aspiring administrators. It was in the middle of a conversation about servant leadership. As I spoke the words in this secular setting (although educators often feel like missionaries), it struck me that the same is true in our spiritual lives.

The Bible says that obedience is better than sacrifice. We often try to be a hero, a martyr for the faith in specific situations. We give a big sum of money for the Christmas family or donate to the orphans in Africa after watching a video. We spend a day or a week doing a high-profile mission adventure. We stuff a shoebox or build a wall. Are these bad? Absolutely not!

We have our moments we follow Christ with all our heart and we let our light shine brightly. But, we often do not stay charged and frequently fade. What is more effective and far more difficult requires more dedication and only happens over time is to be solar-powered. That is, we should be charged by the Son.

Instead of taking a one-time stand and slaying dragons and trying to be a hero, Christ calls us to be faithful, to build a legacy to leave behind.

If you do not believe this, think of the people who have impacted you the most in a positive way. It is most likely someone who consistently showed love. I remember living on the Arkansas border, far from our family. A precious lady showed up on our doorstep multiple times during the the three years we lived there with a fresh loaf of bread, still warm from the oven. She never stayed for more than a few minutes as she had other loaves to deliver. A precious man from our church mows a widow's lawn every week during the growing season. A security guard's wife bakes cookies for the football team all through the season. A couple I know volunteered at a local pregnancy center for three years before I ever knew. There are a thousand other examples of friends who call and check on each other during hard times, bunko groups who clean a member's home when she has a death in the family, Sunday School teachers who send a hand-written note, and on and on.

As Christians, we are called to be solar-powered to have a constant energy from the Son. By living out our faith in obedience, we build a foundation that becomes a legacy.

CHALLENGE: Take inventory. What are you right with the wrong motives? What are you called to do in obedience? Go and Do!

Day 33

Selfishness

VERSE: Philippians 2:3: "Do nothing out of selfish ambition or vain conceit, but in humility consider others better than yourselves."

This morning at church, I stopped to talk to a friend who seemed troubled, as she was on the verge of tears. As she talked, she suddenly stopped to apologize and said she was sorry she made it "all about her" and that she was being selfish. Although that thought never crossed my mind during our conversation, it made me think about how many times I find myself in the same situation - making life all about me. There are moments I sincerely want life to be all about me in a selfish manner. That stings a little.

The first three times I started reading "The Purpose Driven Life", I stopped after the first sentence. "It's not about all you." That sentence was convicting enough! (I have subsequently read this excellent book twice.) We do, though, don't we? We make life all about ourselves!!! Selfishness is demonstrated many ways:

<u>Consuming Conversations</u>. Take a self-assessment. Do you genuinely care about others by asking and engaging them in a two-way conversation? Or do you consume a conversation with your news, your problems, your complaints, your achievements?

<u>Worry</u>. When we focus on our problems and spend unnecessary time worrying instead of trusting, we are selfish.

<u>Bragging</u>. When we focus on our own accomplishments and talents or even those of our children and grandchildren, we put the spotlight on

ourselves. That is selfish. It is also dangerous as it puts our lives under a microscope.

Low self-esteem. There are highs and lows in life. When we focus on our negative situations and problems, that is exactly what we will find. It is the opposite of bragging but it is still a total focus on ourselves and is, you guessed it, selfish.

Unmotivated Giving. Many times we find ourselves giving sparingly and grudgingly. That is because giving of our times, talents or money takes away from ourselves. When we do not give or give with a grumbling spirit, it is out of selfishness and thinking ourselves more important than others.

I am so glad that God was not selfish with His love for me. He was not selfish with His forgiveness, His mercy and grace, His promise to give me a future. He gave His very life out of complete UNselfishness.

CHALLENGE: Look at your calendar, your text messages, your checkbook - are you selfish??

Day 34

The Fear of Success

VERSE: Joshua 1:7: "Be strong and very courageous. Be careful to obey all the laws my servant Moses gave you; do not turn from it to the right or to the left, that you may be successful wherever you go."

I do not know about you, but truthfully I am not really awesome at anything. I am not a great singer or a seamstress or a natural at sports. We are a family that has our hands in various activities, but we are not the MVPs of our chosen pursuits. Then, we discovered the Pinewood Derby race in Cub Scouts. Much research was done, many hours were invested in tweaking the little factors to perfect the car, scores of prototypes were drawn to have the coolest cars, and a quest for the fastest car was underway. We participated for five years. The first year, we had a surprise 2nd place win. Second place means the first loser, so my guys were bound and determined to win the derby the next year.

After a couple years of winning, people began to talk. Sometimes people asked what the secrets were and sometimes their comments bordered on being rude. In year 5, knowing it was our last year of competition, we tried to decide if we were going to give it our best shot or if we were going to bow out and pass the baton. After some discussion, we decided to try our best. In a world where everyone gets a trophy, we have almost become fearful of success. It is easier to be mediocre so that we do not bring negative attention to ourselves. There is a sense it is "lonely at the top". If we made a conscious decision to TRY to fail, we were not teaching our boys to ALWAYS do their best.

I must say that there was a sense of guilt as the boys received their trophies. We had a long discussion about winning and losing with grace and humility. It was a good lesson for all of us.

There are times we choose not to engage in activities because we are afraid we will fail. And, there are times we choose not to engage because we are afraid to succeed. I see this in education - students are sometimes afraid they will succeed in school and not be perceived as "cool' or be accepted by the neighborhood kids. Some will not pursue their love of music because dad expects them to play football. The list goes on and on.

I am glad that God did not have a fear of success. He sent His Son, knowing He would change the world. Yes, people were rude and cruel. They hurled insults and nailed him to a cross. His human nature said, "Let this cup pass from me" because He knew full well that success is difficult. His Spirit said, "not my will, but YOURS be done" because He knew the ultimate result of His success would be worth it in the end. He was on a mission to save the world.

We should always show humility. We should be gracious always (because we KNOW how it feels to lose). We should never be obnoxious. But, God does not call us to be fearful of success. Never quit trying.

CHALLENGE: Make a list of activities in which you are involved. What are you good at? Are you giving it your best?

Day 35

I told you so!!!

VERSE: Genesis 50:20: "You intended to harm me, but God intended it for good to accomplish what is now being done, the saving of many lives."

Imagine being taken away and dropped in a place with no Bible, no "verse of the day" on your iPad, no encouraging words on Facebook or Twitter, no devotion books, no contact with people of faith. That is exactly what happened when Joseph, the beloved first son of Jacob and Rachel when he was sold into slavery by his brothers. When he entered Egypt, he entered a land of spiritual darkness.

He was 17 years old and apparently voiced the words of a 1980's Amy Grant song in his spirit. "I have decided I'm gonna live like a believer, turn my back on the deceiver, I'm gonna live what I believe." Joseph had the ability to have long-distance sight. He saw past the mountain tops of being showered with gifts such as the coat of many colors and being a top administrator in Potipher's regime. He saw past the valleys of slavery and being imprisoned for 13 years for a crime he did not commit. He saw past it all to the shining horizon of God's divine promises. Throughout his life, he had an unwavering faith that God would keep His promise to Abraham.

In a turn of events only God could orchestrate, there was a famine for which Egypt was prepared through Joseph's dream interpretation. Joseph's family needed food. As they stood before Joseph, he realized they also needed forgiveness. He moved all 66 family members to the palace to take care of those who had previously betrayed him.

On his deathbed of 100 years, he spoke of the Exodus of God's people out of Egypt and gave instructions about his bones. He still believed God would keep His promise. Fast forward scores of years! Moses took his bones out of Egypt, headed to the promised land. During the processional of Joseph's bones, it was as if to say, "I told you so! I told you that God ALWAYS keeps His promises". It may not be on our timetable, but He never lies! Joseph lived a life of faith, regardless of his roller-coaster of circumstances.

Oh, that I would see past my own personal mountains and valleys and see the shining horizon of His divine promises.

CHALLENGE: Google Steve Green's song, "He who began a good work in you" and let it seep into your spirit!

Day 36

An 8 oz bottle of water

VERSE: Psalm 42:1: "As the deer pants for streams of water, so my soul pants for you, Oh God."

I have been training for a half marathon. I have done lots of them. Training looks a lot different when you are 40 with kids going in all directions with a job that keeps you on your toes, and is more challenging than it was 15 years ago. I have been working to stay on track.

Last week my long run was 12 and it felt GREAT!!!!! Like, seriously, the weather was perfect, my legs felt great, etc. Today, my long run was 10. Should be a piece of cake, right? Well I was struggling to be honest! It was warmer than I thought it would be and I had not drank enough water. And, I simply ran out of gas. I did not eat enough before I ran, or even the day before. Then, I ran the first 4 miles at a minute's pace faster than normal. About mile 6 I was ready to crash and burn. I talked to myself and wondered why in the WORLD I even wanted to do this. It was tough. I was tired. Everything hurt. I was frustrated because this was easy last week! I mean, six miles is good, right? Maybe I should just call it a day. My mind ran in a thousand different directions oscillating between stopping and continuing. I stopped to walk for a minute and was wrestling with myself as to whether I was going to throw in the towel for the day. About that time, a truck pulled into a driveway in front of me and held out an 8 oz bottle of water. It could NOT have come at a better time. It gave me nourishment that I needed to push through the last few miles.

As I ran, I thought about myself in a different light. Sometimes my spiritual life is right on track. It is natural to follow His will. Other times, though, it is a struggle. Even when it is an easier "situation". Why???? Just like I needed nourishment to finish a ten mile run, I need nourishment to run the course of life. Just like I needed that bottle of water, I need the Living Water to nourish my soul. The Living Water comes through the Word, spending time with Him and mediating on the ideals of God. Nourishment comes in the quietness of my heart and is built on a relationship with Him.

As you run your life's course, be sure to drink from the Living Water and stay nourished by feasting on manna from heaven. It will make ALL the difference!!!

CHALLENGE: Do you feel like you are running on empty spiritually? If so, ask yourself if you are receiving the nourishment you need from His Word. If not, drink up!

Day 37

The Three Rules

VERSE: 1 Thessalonians 2:7: "We were gentle among you, like a mother caring for her little children."

Whoever said taking your kids to kindergarten was hard lied. I did not have one single problem taking my boys to our awesome school. I knew the teacher and was excited because I knew all the fun lessons they would learn. We carefully picked our our "first day of school" clothes. We had our monogrammed bags and snacks packed. We talked about the excitement all morning and hopped in the car and cheerfully sang, "The Cartoon Song" (our favorite at the time). They were excited and I was excited to see them excited. We were all smiles. We walked down the hall and they found their classroom. They located their hook for their bag and their seat with their name on it. There on the table was a prize bag from the teacher and a coloring sheet. Smiles all around!!! I paid for their lunch ticket and chatted with the teacher for just a second. This was a piece of cake. I win mom-of-the-year. Then, I had to leave. Leave???? Can I not just stay and watch them play with the toys, read in the loft, make new friends, interact with the teacher?? I will be perfectly quiet. Oh, but no! I had to leave. So, THIS is the hard part. The hall never seemed so long nor the steps of the school so steep. Somehow, I ambled to my car, put the key in the ignition and ended up in a grocery store parking lot (maybe my car was on auto-pilot). I buried my head in the steering wheel and just cried. Not the pretty movie-star cry either!

In the next few moments, I allowed myself to be sad that my boys were growing up. The moment they stepped over the threshold of the school seemed like they crossed a rite of passage. If that was the case, then I had to do the same. I had to step up and be a mom of school-age kiddos. I prayed about how to articulate to them everything God had in store for them, how I wanted them to treat others, what was in front of them academically, how to deal with unfriendly people, and how to focus on what matters.

That afternoon, I listened incessantly as they talked about their day and all the neat activities they had done. I listened with moistened eyes. What also emerged from that conversation was a conversation about rules. They told me the class rules and how you could "get your clothespin moved". It was intense. I told them we needed some life rules. After a bit of chatter, we came up with 3. Work hard, do your best, and have a good attitude. We recited these rules every day for the next couple years. We talked about what they mean in certain situations. We talked about how to have a good attitude when someone questioned their faith. We talked about what it means to work hard when the teacher asks you to show your work and you knew the answer "in your head". Even now, many years later, we re-visit those rules. We apply them to lots of situations in the here and now. I am glad that we stopped for a moment to grasp on to a system that do not contain rules for a moment, but for a lifetime.

Work hard. Do your best. Have a good attitude!

CHALLENGE: What are YOUR life rules? Think about what actions you want to show the world.

Day 38

What we do MATTERS!!!

VERSE: 1 Corinthians 10:31: "So whether you eat or drink or whatever you do, do it all for the glory of God."

There are days I feel insignificant. It seems my days are spent doing chores and working hard to cross everything off my "to do" list. Does all this really make a difference? Some days I feel insecure. My feelings are on edge and the least little thing topples my self-image. I see that other people seem to have it all together and I am trying to remember if I brushed my teeth this morning. Some days, I even feel invisible. Does anybody see me - or just the tasks I do? There are times I lay my head down and wonder if what I do even really matters. Maybe you have had those days, too.

However, there are days when I am certain God winks at me. If I am faithful to seek His face, there are moments when the nuggets of the truth seep out of my pores and spill onto others. Sometimes I put reminders on my phone to pray for someone or a particular situation. Such is the case with a friend of mine. At the allotted time, I sent her a text that I prayed for comfort. She sent a message back saying it was the first time in over a week she did not have a particular health issue. That same afternoon, I was asked to speak at a professional conference, and the director specifically asked me to tell my "Be Still and Know" story because it had previously made a difference to her.

People have said and performed random acts of kindness for you that truly make a difference. You have received a call, a letter, or a card on a day you needed it the most. You have gotten a visit when your thoughts were dark. During a long period of infertility, I received some bad lab results. I was at the end of my rope. A precious nurse with no good answers to give, simply quoted scripture over me.

We often neglect being a difference because we do not know the right words to say, because we are busy, because we have our own difficulties. God has called us to do everything for HIS glory. Whether we work in retail, business, education, domestic engineering....whether we are cleaning toilets or speaking with the president....what we DO matters!!!! People may not notice anything more than our attitude. As we let the nuggets of His truth seep into our pores, they will spill onto others.

And, it makes all the difference!!!

CHALLENGE: Do not have a pity party over your own trials? Find 3 ways to bless others today. Then, praise God for providing YOU with the blessing.

$\mathcal{D}ay\ 39$

The waters never part
until your feet get wet

VERSE: Hebrews 11:29: "By faith the people passed through the Red Sea as on dry land; but when the Egyptians tried to do so, they were drowned."

Around 1990, a group named Petra released a Christian rock song, Beyond Belief, that contains the line, "the waters never part until your feet get wet." This is in reference to Exodus 14 when the people of Israel were faced with a dilemma. After the ten plagues in Egypt, the Pharaoh told Moses that he and his people could GO! Shortly there after, he changed his mind and sent his army after Moses and the Hebrew people. After all they had been through, the people of Israel found themselves trapped humanly speaking. On one side was an impassable mountain range; on the other side were in-survivable sand dunes; behind them was the army of Pharaoh; and in front of them was the Red Sea. They cried out in anger toward Moses as to why he would lead them all this way just to die. God told Moses to stretch out his rod and the waters would part for them to cross through the Red Sea. And, they did!

Have you ever felt trapped? Like, there was no way humanly speaking to escape a situation? We sometimes feel the world closing in on us from every side. We, like the Hebrew children, cry out and complain. God goes before us and has a way of escape prepared for us, if only we will have faith.

God gave a command to Moses, but the Israelites had to step out in faith. They would never have reached the other side had they not taken the first step. Because of that step, God protected His people and provided one of the greatest miracles in the Bible.

As you find yourself penned in a seemingly impossible situation, stand still and listen for God's command. He has a plan that you cannot even fathom. He will bring people across your path that you never expected, He will open doors you were unaware even existed, He will perform a miracle so you have no choice but to look up and know He gave you a special touch. Then, obey His voice. He will do immeasurably more than you can ever imagine.

Do not be afraid of wet toes!

CHALLENGE: What are your struggles right now? Where do you feel trapped? Instead of looking all around you at the impossibilities, look UP to the Possibility, to the Promise!

$\mathcal{D}ay$ 40

Sunshine

VERSE: 2 Samuel 23:4: "He is like the light of morning at sunrise on a cloudless morning, like the brightness after rain that brings the grass from the earth."

The term "sunshine" has several meanings in my life. My biological father always called me Sunshine. Even though we did not see each other often after age 3, that is how cards and letters were always addressed and are even today. I have a propensity to make a song out of everything. It seems to make the day go by brighter. A friend made a comment one day, and I sang, "You are my sunshine, my only sunshine." You know the rest and you are smiling as you sing it. This became our theme song during a particularly troubling time at work. It was the signal that, "hey, I could use a ray of sunshine right now and I know God will speak a word through you". It was accountability and encouragement all rolled into one. Still, to this day, we see who can out-do each other on finding a "sunshine" item for Christmas. Another friend periodically sends an e-mail or Facebook message that says, "BE the sunshine". After attending a conference several years ago, she made it her mission to spur on believers to remember WHOSE we are and WHO we represent.

I have often wondered why God chose to put some many rays of sunshine in my pathway. Is it because of my shining personality or because I can be a little cloudy some days? What I have realized is - BOTH! Just like those winter months that cause us to lose our spunk because of the lack of the sun's rays, we can become cloudy and dreary when we lack being in the SON's rays. It is great to have people in my life who remind me the let the SON peek through the clouds. After all, even the clouds look better when the sun shines through. When the sky is full of clouds, all we see is a dreary day. However, nothing beats an afternoon of lying on your back with a child and seeing shapes in the clouds. That is how much the sun changes our perspective. The same is true for our troubles. When we let the SON shine through, it certainly changes the look of our problems.

Then, there are times that I need to let MY let shine to others. Just because I am on the mountain top does not mean that my closest friends are standing beside me. They may be trudging up the hill I just climbed. My job then becomes to BE a reflection the light to break through their way along the journey.

I guess my Dad did not name me Sunshine on accident all those years ago. God had a bigger lesson in store for me.

CHALLENGE: Check the weather inside your soul. Are you partly cloudy? Is there a fog over your life? Or are you letting the rays of the Son shine through?

Day 41

Trusting Him

VERSE: Jeremiah 29:11: "For I know the plans I have for you," declares The Lord, "plans to prosper you and not harm you, plans to give you a hope and a future."

Sometimes I like to help God. He needs my help. After all, He has billions of people to attend to on a daily basis. There are needs all over the world, and at any given moment, there are millions of people who desperately need His touch. When I find myself in a tough situation or am unsure about a decision coming my way, I pray. Often in my prayers, I will give God some solutions to the dilemma. Even if it is in my mind, I will offer my sincerest advice on how God can fix my particular situation of the moment.

However, sometimes God neglects to take my advice. There are times He gives me far more than I could ever have imagined. And, there are times God says, "no". There have been many times in my life that I questioned those times. I have been sad; I have been angry with God; I have felt like He simply wasn't listening to my prayers; I have wondered if He had forgotten me; I have wondered if I listened to the wrong voice; I have been in the place of simply NOT understanding.

On the other hand, I am quick to say I trust God and am committed to wanting His will for my life. When others are going through a difficult time or are facing an uncertain dilemma I offer words of faith, encouraging others to trust His will above all. There are have been times I heard the words I spoke with fresh ears because they are the very words I need to hear in my soul.

Several years ago, I put an end to this tug-of-war in my spirit with one simple statement. "I cannot say I trust Him if I only trust Him when He gives me what I want."

How profound!!!! I tend to say, "I am blessed" when life goes well, and pout when I struggle. The truth is - I am always blessed! And, I can ALWAYS trust Him. He has my best interest at heart in both the good times and the bad times. There are many situations I pray for the wrong answer because I do not have His perspective. If He said "yes" to all my whims, He would not be the omniscient God that He is.

As I pray and seek His will, I will stop giving advice and asking God to simply bless my will. I will trust Him - in times He gives me what I want AND in times I get the exact opposite. If I do not trust Him ALL the time, then I trust Him NONE of the time. His promises are true, and His love never fails.

I can trust Him. Always!

CHALLENGE: Listen to your prayers. Do you find yourself talking more than listening? Do you struggle with wondering if God is there when you do not get what you want? Ask yourself if you TRULY trust Him or if you are asking Him to simply bless what you have already decided.

Day 42

Quiet Please

VERSE: Proverbs 17:28: "Even a fool is thought wise if he keeps silent, and discerning if he holds his tongue."

Today, I attended a meeting. During all three sessions, there were people around me chatting during the main speakers. To be honest, it drove me crazy! I even turned around a couple times with my best "teacher look". Even this did not stop the constant noise. The speakers were phenomenal and I was desperately trying to glean from their knowledge. They had important information to provide and I had ears to hear. The voices all around me were quite distracting. Honestly, there were times I listened to their conversations, hoping they would be something of substance. Maybe they were discussing how to implement the strategies into their local situations. They were not. There were times I tried diligently to focus on the speaker's voice and focus on his words, even writing down important points that were addressed. I even scribbled a note to the friend on my left stating how frustrating it was for adults to be so rude during a presentation. It felt better to complain a little. Well, not really. I whispered to the friend on my right, then realizing I was becoming just like the people about whom I was complaining. After several tactics, the voices were still there and I still could not focus on the speaker. I finally removed myself from that spot. I moved to a different area where the attendees were paying attention. What a relief! I was finally able to focus and to acquire the information I so greatly desired.

You see the parallel right? Think about our relationship with God. He is the main speaker and He has the wisdom we need. He is ready and willing to share His wisdom with us, collectively and individually. We live in a world full of all kinds of voices. We have monetary aspirations, career goals, travel plans, insecurities, varied friendships, and busy schedules pulling us in every direction. It often makes it difficult to focus. We have moments we look at these distractors and roll our eyes, knowing we should pay closer attention to the One who matters. We complain about being busy, about where our priorities lie, and some toxic friendships. Sometimes we even listen to the voices to see if there is negativity we think we need to hear - Is my co-worker talking behind my back? Is there more to life than cleaning toilets? Why am I going through a hard time? How will I juggle the five entries on the calendar tomorrow? I wonder......what if......when...where..who.how??

But, there comes a time when we have to remove ourselves from the voices that pull us away from the One voice we need to hear. We have to step away and find ourselves with a little "quiet" so that we can hear His voice. Once we do, it is amazing what we will hear. We will hear the very words that soothe our souls and take us to a place of peace! Life is full of voices that are willing to pull us here and there. We have to be willing to strategically find ourselves in a place of "quiet" so that we can receive wisdom and stay rejuvenated to focus on what truly matters!

CHALLENGE: Take inventory of the thoughts that keep you up at night. Are those thoughts jumbled and focused in many directions or do you fall asleep peacefully, knowing you have spent time focusing on the One voice that truly matters?

Day 43

You DO exist....

VERSE: 1 John 3:2: "Dear friends, now we are children of God, and what we will be has not yet been made known. But we know that when he appears, we shall be like him, for we shall see him as he is."

One of my favorite commercials during Christmas is when the red M&M and Santa meet and both pass out, exclaiming, "You DO exist!" A similar incident happened at church this morning. We had a new Student Minister join our staff about a month ago, whose Search Committee I was on. Over the time beginning with his initial Skype interview and the process of local visits, we became friends. But, since he has been on staff, we have not seen one another in church. I was sick one week; he was on a Senior Ski trip another week and we simply did not cross paths. This morning, we passed on our journey to the balcony. He gave me a hug and exclaimed, "You DO exist!"

What would make one say those words? "You DO exist." It is a relationship, a personal encounter. It is the difference between knowing and believing, the difference between head knowledge and heart knowledge, the ultimate difference between religion and a relationship.

Santa and the M&M had heard of one another and likely knew stories of one another's existence and antics, a little folklore. However, when they came face-to-face, there was no denying their existence. A sort of reverence occurred. The same is true with God. Likely, we have all heard stories. From Sunday School to Vacation Bible School to sitting at our grandmother's knee, we have heard stories about Noah's

Ark, the parting of the Red Sea, the Virgin Birth, the empty tomb, and the splendors of Heaven. We may even live by the Ten Commandments, exhibit the Fruit of the Spirit, and apply the Beatitudes. We may have a knowledge of historical times during the life and legacy of Christ.

Until we have a personal encounter with God, it is folklore. Beyond the stories and past the lessons and sermons we hear, we must have a face-to-face moment when we realize deep in our soul that He DOES exist! When we truly see Him for who He is, a reverence occurs. When we realize who He is, we realize who we are and our need for His love, His guidance, His discipline, His protection, and His ultimate Salvation!

Once we realize He does exist in a real way, we will never be the same again. Just like we cannot un-see a picture or un-hear a word, we will never un-know that God does exist once we have truly encountered Him. We may deny or choose a different path, but we will always know that The Lord, He is God! We will know that He DOES exist!

CHALLENGE: Are the stories of the Bible folklore to you or have you had a personal encounter of His existence? Stop now and seek His face!

$\mathcal{D}ay$ 44

Substitutes

VERSE: Exodus 20:3: "You shall have no other gods before me."

Every morning for years, I had the same routine. I tapped my alarm clock, took a shower, brushed my teeth, drew lines on my eyelids and lips, packed backpacks and gym bags. Then, I popped a top on a can of diet soda. I needed caffeine! Those around me needed me to have that caffeine. I loved the tickle in my throat and the little "wake up" it provided. Over the years, I drank more and more diet soda until it was almost exclusively my drink of choice. Until one day, I realized I was relying on a "substitute" to fill a need. I needed energy and the soda gave me a temporary lift, but I always needed more because I was never truly satisfied.

Don't we do that? Try to fill our voids with "substitutes"? We look to many material belongings and activities to make us happy - nice houses, busy kids, prestige, relationships, accolades, vices, shopping, honors for our children and grandchildren, eating, negative people / drama, performance, exercise, status, and the list could go on and on. We are never truly satisfied, are we? I mean REALLY satisfied! That is because these undertakings are a substitute for what REALLY matters.

In Sunday School, we have been studying Hebrews 11, the Great Hall of Faith. Look at verse 1: "Faith is the substance of things hoped for, the evidence of things not seen." Faith (the demonstration of our salvation) is the substance (the valid, significant, most essential part of something; tangible; solid) of the deepest longings of our heart (not our wants - but the deep parts of our very souls) and the evidence (indicators that are obvious to the eye and mind; visible signs, something that makes plain and clear) of what we have not (yet) seen. Why is not yet clear? Because we see life from the wrong side of heaven. We are still seeing the underside of the tapestry of our lives.

I reached a place in which I no longer wanted a substitute and started drinking water. It was tough at first, but then it was fabulous! Health issues cleared up and I found I had MORE energy than before.

That is exactly how it is with our faith. When we stop filling our lives with substitutes and replace them with what is REAL - which is a deep relationship with Christ - it is fabulous! The shift is sometimes difficult at first, but the rewards are incredible. No guilt! We begin to know His power and His peace!

CHALLENGE: Write down how you spend your time mentally. What are areas you are using substitutes to fill an emptiness that only Christ can fill? As you take inventory, be honest. This is the first step in changing habits!

Day 45

The Desert

VERSE: I John 2:16: "For everything in the world – the cravings of sinful man, the lust of his eyes, and the boasting of what he has and does – comes not from the Father, but from the world."

Today, we attended a sister church in town to celebrate Scout Sunday to show appreciation for the church's sponsorship and support for a program for our children. The pastor began a series leading up to Easter entitled, "The Path" which will take stops along the Path of Christ. Today's sermon dealt with the temptation of Jesus in the wilderness. The pastor did a superb job of describing the devil's temptation and the appropriate responses of Jesus. In the middle, he made a statement that stuck with me and rattled around in my brain for many hours. The statement was, "We never know who we really are until we have spent some time in the desert."

You know, there is a lot of truth in that statement. When life is going well, it is easy to be a person of character and to maintain our faith and to choose right over wrong. However, we have all had times of struggle - when we are tempted to give in to "wrong", to try to be someone we aren't, to relinquish control over to what seems an easier choice. Those moments only lead to emptiness. We will all surely have those times in our lives when we are in the wilderness. What separates us is how we handle temptation during those times. During our seasons of struggle, the enemy knows our weak spots and will try to tempt us to step away from the truth - through lusts of the flesh (the offer of pampering), the

Janice M. Stockman

lusts of the eyes (the offer of perishables) and the pride of life (the offer of position). The greatest way to resist the devil is through the words from the Scripture.

You are either coming out of a desert situation, in the midst of the desert, or will be headed in that direction. The devil will tempt you in the same way he did Jesus. He will tempt you with lusts of the flesh (pampering the appetite, indulging), lusts of the eyes (material belongings, worldly pleasures), and the pride of life (honor, vain conceit, selfishness). As you are there do not despair. God is steady by your side and will walk you through the most difficult of times. These are the moments that truly define us. Stay Strong!

CHALLENGE: Have you ever memorized scripture? If not, I encourage you to commit to learning five verses. That way, when you face temptations, you are armed with truth. Write them on index cards, tape them on your mirror, and hide the words in your heart.

Are you in it for the INcome
or the OUTcome?

VERSE: 1 Corinthians 15:58: "Therefore, my brothers, stand firm. Let nothing move you. Always give yourself fully to the work of The Lord, because you know that your labor for The Lord is not in vain."

I know a precious lady who works as a Special Education teacher for high school students. This is often quite tricky as teenagers do not want people to realize they are "different". Often, teens who have struggled for many years give in to the lie that they are less of a person because they are not as academically capable as their peers. Sometimes this shows up in misbehavior and in difficult times managing school and life. Dealing with this day in and day out takes its toll. The paperwork mounts too high, the phone calls are too many to return, the expectations are overwhelming. This wonderful teacher was ready to throw in the towel. More importantly, she questioned whether she was doing the right thing - if anything she did even mattered. You have those days. Sometimes they stretch into weeks or months and you question what your purpose is.

Fast forward several months. We had a football signing for several students who had received scholarships. In the South, football is a big deal!! One by one, the guys went to the signing table, gave appropriate thanks to their families, coaches, and friends for their support. They announced the college they would attend, slipped on a cap with their new logo, and signed their intent. It really is an exciting time for these fellows. After they sign, parents and family members come up to the table for pictures. Then, teachers and coaches are encouraged to come for the next set of pictures. However, no teachers joined the ranks....only the coaches. The last guy was one who had struggled to make it through four years of high school. Simply reaching this point was monumental. Over the past four years, he had developed into an incredible young man. He went through the same routine. Except that he motioned for his Special Education teacher to sit right beside him with all the coaches as he signed to go to a junior college a couple states away.

With two flicks of a wrist, it changed her entire attitude. She cried. I cried watching the scene unfold. Before hundreds of people, she was the only teacher who was called up by one of the guys. Everyone knew she was a Special Education teacher. He did not care because he knew what it had taken to arrive at this place.

Her paperwork pile was just as high. The phone calls were just as numerous. The expectations kept rising. She remembered that she was in this business for the OUTcome. INcome is nice, but making a difference is simply priceless.

CHALLENGE: No matter your job or place in life, you have the opportunity to make a difference! Do not focus on what your INcome is. Focus on what you can do to have a positive OUTcome for others. In the midst of that, you will find yourself incredibly blessed!

Day 47

When you come to the place I'm all you have, you'll find I'm all you need

VERSE: 2 Corinthians 12:9a: "My grace is sufficient for you, for my power is made perfect in weakness."

When I was about ten years old, we went to a small church. We knew every person who attended, and everyone participated in everything. It was the church where I learned about serving God and where I learned to eat oysters and where my brother learned that eating all the gumdrops from the gumdrop tree really will make you sick. There are many great memories from our years there. My mom often played the piano, and one day at home while she was practicing, I sang along with her. She asked if I would like to sing in church. That conversation led to my first solo. I sang an old favorite, "Lean on Me." I practiced about 2,349 times because I was nervous. I did not want to forget my words in front of everyone. Because I practiced so many times, those words have been forever forged into my heart as an etching.

"Lean on me....when you have no place to stand....when you feel you're going under, hold tighter to my hand....Lean on me....when your heart begins to bleed....when you come to the place that I'm all you have, you'll find I'm all you need."

Fast forward twenty years. We were in the midst of a fertility battle, one in which we were losing profusely. We had been to doctors, we had prayed, we had multiple procedures. I could not understand why God did not want us to have children. My emotions were all over the place at times. Baby showers were difficult, and I almost cried when people would ask why we did not have any children yet. One particular instance will stick with me forever. About three and a half years into the five year journey, I got a phone call at school. I received the message to call the nurse as she had some lab results for me. During my planning time, I went to the front office to return the call. My principal said I could use his office to have some privacy. The call did not go well as she gave me some bad lab results. My soul and my spirit were exhausted. I do not even know that I had the strength to be angry. I sat on the floor and began to cry. This precious nurse had to listen to me as I was at the very end of my rope. Then, she did something I will never forget. She did not make a promise that everything would be okay. She did not give me false hope. She simply began to quote scripture over me. Over and over and over. They were HIS words, not hers. I went from a place of feeling like I would never get off that floor (nor did I much care if I did) to a place of contentment, knowing I was not forgotten. At the end of the conversation, she told me I had reached the place where HE was all I had, and now I could know HE was all I needed. The words of that song came flooding back and I sang them over and over until I could walk out of that office, knowing - no matter what - I was okay because I was His.

I imagine you have been at that place - or maybe you are at that place now. Let those words wash over you until you know that your circumstances will not define you.

CHALLENGE: Look at YouTube and find that old song, "Lean on Me" (not the 1972 Bill Withers song). Listen to the words and let them sink into your soul. You may not need them today, but the day you do need them will be one you will never forget.

$\mathcal{D}ay$ 48

Graduations and Marathons

VERSE: Hebrews 12:1: "Therefore, since we are surrounded by such a great cloud of witnesses, let us throw off everything that hinders and the sin that so easily entangles, and let us run with perseverance the race marked out for us."

The year that I moved my office to a high school was eye-opening! I suddenly worked in the midst of over 2,000 teenagers, all of whom were taller than me (well, except for one and that is why she is my favorite). They were big kids and little adults and I never knew which side of them I would get on any certain day. Learning a new school with new administration, moving from elementary to secondary curriculum, hearing all new vocabulary words like "credits" and "units" and "diploma options" and "four-year plans", and dealing with the daily schedule of moving over 2,000 children seven times a day was a bit overwhelming. I watched students who struggled at times, but they kept going and never quit. On rough days, they would sometimes come to my office and we would talk through their frustration with a teacher or over a project or how to deal with their peers. We often talked about making right choices. Of course, there were some I built relationships with over the year, and prayed for a little more regularly than others. In late May, we have a little ceremony called Graduation. Almost 500 students lined up in rows with matching caps and gowns. The arena was filled with parents and grandparents and friends and loved ones. There was excitement in the air as the familiar march began to play. Then, came the time to call each name. Our theatre director spoke succinctly for each child as they they walked across the stage to receive their diploma. I have the privilege of being on stage with them and shaking hands as they walk across. I got many hugs from some incredible children. Some of them received scholarships to colleges and some barely scraped by. But for all of them, this was their day! They had done what it took to cross the finish line.

Since I did not have enough going on, I also decided to run my first marathon that year. Previously, I had run several half marathons, so surely this was not much different. Boy, was I wrong! Training for a full marathon (that is 26.2 miles) took a lot of time and dedication. I had to plan out long runs in advance so that I would be prepared for the end result - the race. I paid my money to secure my spot. For months, I trained to be ready as I steadily increased my mileage. I did speed training once a week. I tried to eat better and drank a lot more water. There were days I wanted to quit, days my family wanted me to to quit, and days I simply hated running. I kept going. The weekend finally arrived. My best friend and I drove up and spent the night. We got up early, ate a bagel and banana, and set off. We made a few memories along the course. Over four hours later, I crossed the finish line. I was not declared the winner because I did not cross first. However, I was a winner because I crossed at all. It was an awesome feeling!

Life is like that. We are in this for the long haul. Some days are tough and we feel like giving up. Press on! For one day, we will stand before God and account for our lives. He will not ask if we crossed the finish line first or if we were the first in our "class". He will ask us if we did the essentials - Confess our sins, Believe in Him, and Ask Him into our heart.

CHALLENGE: Stand strong during the tough days. Just like preparing for a marathon or working toward graduation, there are days you'll struggle. Push through those days and focus on the end prize!

Day 49

Treasure Box

VERSE: Matthew 6:21: "For where your treasure is, there your heart will be also."

When my boys were in the second grade, they made a treasure box and put 10 important items in the box. They decorated it all over with stickers and jewels, and then brought it home with instructions not to open it until high school graduation. I must admit, I peeked. I was surprised at a few of the items they chose. I was surprised they did not have Legos in there because they played with them all the time. My athletic son had a tiny wooden baseball bat keyring to represent his love of sports. The one who loves to read put in a bookmark. They each had a scroll with pictures of specific things they loved. They drew objects like egg sandwiches and grilled burgers. This surprised me, but I realized it was because they valued the time we shared at the dinner table. There were items missing...there was no mention of electronics. As much as they love their devices, they were not in their Top 10 important items. All in all, it did show me what they thought was TRULY important - tokens they wanted to hold onto for a long time. Even though I know my boys pretty well, I was incorrect about a few of the items they chose.

Our heart is like a treasure box. We keep in our heart what is TRULY important to us. Sometimes we show the world what we want them to see and we act like certain activities are really important. That is not always true. When we act like a Christian at church, but not in front of our friends, we are hiding something in our treasure box that we do not want others to see. In the same way, when we go out of way to help others, even when no one notices, we are hiding true gems in our treasure box. God does not look only at our actions, but at the motives of our heart. That is where true treasure lies.

At the end of time, we will stand before God and He will open our treasure box by looking into our heart. What will He find when He sees yours? What treasures will He find? Will He find that your treasures are of this world - popularity, selfishness, pride, disobedience? Or will He find your treasures are found in Him - salvation, mercy, helpfulness, sacrifice, faithfulness?

CHALLENGE: Make a list of 10 attributes you want others to see in you. Now, peek inside your treasure box. Are those the activities that consume your time? Your checkbook? Your mind?

$\mathcal{D}ay\ 50$

Grits, Meals on Wheels, and Thrift Store Dresses

VERSE: Matthew 25:40: "I tell you the truth, whatever you did for one of the least of these brothers of mine, you did for me."

I work with this awesome lady. I have known her for many years, but only casually. I have had the opportunity, however, to work closely with her for the past two years. She came into a situation where we were starting an entirely new program, and an important piece of the puzzle was building a team. In His divine wisdom, God always places people exactly where they need to be. Sometimes He outdoes Himself. She is simply amazing!

Maybe you can relate to me, though. I have the best intentions in the world. I have written more encouraging notes, baked more cookies, hugged more necks, and said more prayers in my mind than should be allowed. It just seems like life is so busy. I want to help others, and will even put entries on my "To Do" list that will help others. But sometimes it seems that life gets in the way of actually accomplishing those tasks.

Over the past two years, I have witnessed what Faith in Action really looks like. I have never seen someone who simply fills a need. To be honest, she sometimes does not really ask. She will simply bring a crockpot of grits for our staff on a Friday morning. She even brings the spoons and bowls. No fanfare. Just grits. Or she will call and tell me to be at her house at a certain time, in which case she will have a pot of soup and cornbread or a pan of homemade mac-n-cheese. She offers to cover morning duty when people are going through a rough time, she drops by the house of a new mom to take her a special cup of coffee, she puts together a binder of easy recipes for newlyweds, she reminds me not to forget to wish so-and-so a Happy Birthday. When one of our students needed a dress for a special Black &White Birthday Bash, she immediately called her friend at a Rethreads Shop. She told her what size and that the dress needed to be black and white and cocktail length. Within an hour, we had the dress at school ready for the student. The list could go on and on and on.

She is retiring this year, much to my personal dismay. The greatest legacy she will leave is that she puts her faith in ACTION! We have all picked up the gauntlet just a little because we see what a difference it makes. She makes us look for opportunities to serve. What a precious gift! When we learn to love like Jesus loved, we will find more happiness and contentment than we know what to do with.

CHALLENGE: Look at your calendar and "To Do" list or think through what you are trying to do. Are acts of kindness in there anywhere? If so, go for it! Make it a priority because you will sprinkle seeds of love all over your path!

Day 51

If you cannot be Positive, be Productive

VERSE: 2 Corinthians 9:6: "Remember this: Whoever sows sparingly will also reap sparingly, and whoever sows generously will also reap generously."

Several years ago, I served as a Behavior Specialist for a school district in Arkansas. It was one of the most incredible jobs I have ever had. We had some really neat opportunities to build a character education program, we worked with all the agencies in town to truly help students be successful through collaboration, we were able to speak to groups of students about making wise choices, and I had the opportunity to meet with students individually to assess and help deal with specific behavior issues. To be honest, there were days that were tough! Some days brought me to my knees. Other days, huge progress was made and it made it all worth it. Then there days that still stick with me all these years later.

There was a high school fellow that was dealt a pretty rough hand in life. He was living in a group home, going to school, and trying to get life back on track. He was very smart and had an awesome artistic ability. Obviously, there were some issues there or we would not be meeting. Once a week he and I chatted about how life was going, problems he was having at school, how to manage his feelings in specific incidents, etc. We practiced how to respond when a teacher asked him to do something he thought was ridiculous. We role-played appropriate comments when a student blurted out something immature in class. One day, he was particularly upset and angry. When he was telling me why, I could tell he was getting more upset just telling me the story. He suddenly stopped and asked if I could locate a broom for him.

A broom? Have you ever had that moment you wondered if maybe you were having a different conversation than the other person? This was surely one such moment! I asked him why and he said he was really angry and needed a broom. Reluctantly, I handed him a broom from the next room, unsure whether he was going to knock out the window or me. To my surprise he started sweeping, furiously at first, and then more calmly. I simply watched. After about five minutes, he sat down and told me the rest of his story and we worked through the situation. I asked him about the sweeping. He said something I will never forget, "If you can't be positive, be productive." He told me he had learned that you cannot always be happy. But, instead of sitting around being depressed or angry or perturbed, he would do something productive and put that energy to work.

I am a little unsure who the most mature one in the room was that day, for those words were truly life-changing. There will be times in all our lives when we do not feel "positive" and life is truly difficult sometimes. Instead of wallowing in our misery, we can get up and DO something. We can even follow God's example. When He saw the depravity of man, He did not curl up on the heavenly sofa, He took action! What great words to live by!

If you cannot be Positive, be Productive!!!

CHALLENGE: Take inventory of yourself. How often do you get upset about something and it takes you to a dark place. The next time that happens, get up and grab a broom. Or write a letter. Or clean a closet. Or visit someone in the hospital. Be productive!

Day 52

Picking up Sticks.....again

VERSE: 2 Chronicles 15:7: "But as for you, be strong and do not give up, for your work will be rewarded."

We live on about three acres of land with lots of trees. I love the trees as they provide shade and a feeling of living in the country. I love to watch the cycle of budding leaves in the spring, the fullness in the summer, the changing colors in the fall, and the bareness of naked trees in the winter. I do not love the sticks. Before my husband cranks up the lawn mower, we have to pick up the sticks.....every time. There are always a few wheel barrows full of sticks. We try to make it a fun family affair - we all go together and load up the wheel barrow and the wagon. Jeff blazes up the fire pit. We sing and act silly sometimes. We grab a bag of marshmallows sometimes. However, I get tired of picking up sticks. WHY do they keep falling? There are a thousand other things I could be doing besides picking up sticks from the same spots that I have picked up before. I complain sometimes even if only in my mind. It just gets tiresome.

Then, the job gets done, we pull the weeds from the flower beds, the lawn gets mowed, and the clippings are blown off the driveway. After a few hours working in the yard we frequently go to the edge in the front yard and admire how great it looks. And it really does. The smell of freshly cut grass lingers in the air, there is the hint of sweat - the kind that is great because it lets you know you have worked hard and earned it, everything is neat and trimmed. There is a sense of happiness in the accomplishment. As the fire dies down from burning the sticks, we sometimes sit around the stone pit and enjoy idle chit-chat and simply enjoy each other's presence.

This whole scene was carried out yesterday. It made me think about my spiritual life. Sometimes, it is hard to do the right thing. It can be tough to continue to do the right thing over and over. We have held our tongue about a person once, but it is hard to keep holding our tongue. Or keep tithing. Or keep eating healthy. Or keep praying. Or keep spending daily time with God. Or keep forgiving. Or keep the faith when there is no job in sight. Or keep believing.

Truthfully, if we do not grown weary in doing good, there will come a time we can look on what God has created, knowing it is good. Our soul may be a little tired but it will be the good kind of tired knowing we have pressed on and not given into the temptations of this world, but have stuck to what we know is true. It is during those moments that we can simply enjoy God's presence. For we know that He holds everything in His hands and that He loves us immensely. Even if we have to keep picking up sticks. Those moments draw us closer to Him, keep us in check as to who is in control, create lifetime memories, and give us a glimpse of heavenly accomplishment.

CHALLENGE: No matter what your current situation is - do NOT give up. Keep picking up the sticks, even if you have picked them up a thousand times before. The reward is around the corner, and the payoff is the preciousness of enjoying intimacy with Him!!!

Day 53

Why won't I just play Pirates?

VERSE: Romans 7:15: "I do not understand what I do. For what I want to do I do not do, but what I hate I do."

My boys are boys! They love to play and play and play! They are forever saying, "Mom, come look at this." "Mom, does this Lego piece look good right here?" "Mom, I have created a new superhero superpower!" "Mom, can you help me with this?" "Mom, where is the tiny black round Lego piece that goes in this specific spot that I have looked for only for 20 seconds but I am sure you can find it even though you have no idea what it looks like?" Okay...maybe the last one was my interpretation of the question! You understand my point. If you have children or have ever been around children, you know exactly what I mean.

Sometimes they fail to recognize that the sock and underwear fairy does not live at our house. They forget I have a full-time job, still have to cook dinner, pack baseball clothes, fill out field trip forms, balance the checkbook, scrub the toilets, and ask my husband about his day. If at all possible, I would love to squeeze in a 3-mile run to keep my body (and mind) healthy so I can continue to maintain this routine.

The other day, I was loading the dishwasher and one of the boys came in and asked me to play pirates with him. In my mind, I rolled my eyes thinking I would love to, but these dishes will not wash themselves. I told him I would love to, but needed to finish a few chores first. One thing lead to another and it was bedtime and no pirate action had occurred. I apologized as I lay in his bed for a few minutes. He smiled and said he knew I had a lot to do. Instantly, I was convicted!!! Clean cups are not more important than that face and the precious few years I have him at home. Just play pirates!!! There is nothing better than loving in the moment. I have never once felt guilty for playing a game with them or spending time with them. Why, then, do I get bogged down in temporal preoccupations?

I felt convicted as a mom and as a believer. I often treat God the same way. I will spend time with Him when I finish my list. One thing leads to another and the time has flitted in the wind. There is so much work to be done, and I act as if life cannot continue unless I burn my candle at both ends. This leads to feelings of guilt as I lay in bed and life gets eerily quiet. Nothing is more important than spending time with Him - not a clean house, not a good job at work, not being superwoman, and not even doing church work or performing good deeds. Never once have I felt guilty for spending time with God. Why, then, do I get bogged down in temporal preoccupations? In obsessions that do not matter in the end?

So, here's to making time for Him a priority. It is amazing how everything else falls in place when I take care of first things first!

CHALLENGE: You have heard it a million times. Start your day with some time with God. Everyone is different, but carve out time for Him. You will NOT regret it. Put it on your calendar, put an alarm on your phone, tie a ribbon around your finger, DO something! It will make all the difference!!

Day 54

Fellowship of the Engorged

VERSE: Galatians 5:13: "Do not use your freedom to indulge in the sinful nature; rather, serve one another in love."

I have read many good books and how to put "feet to the Word" books and done lots of Bible Studies about being "on mission' and gone to lots of camps and retreats that encourage a mission component and have friends that are missionaries and sponsor children through organizations and tithe to my church and buy gifts for Christmas families and served at a Children's camp and gone on mission trips.

However I read a book that has altered my way of thinking a bit. The book is *Same Kind of Different as Me* (Ron Hall, 2006). It is an incredible true story of a "chance meeting" of a wealthy art dealer and a 20-year homeless man. They met because the art dealer's wife wanted to SERVE God - not just throw some money at a charity. I am working on letting the words seep in my soul. Then I read the sequel - *What Difference Do it Make?* This is collection of snippets of happenings after the release of the book - lives that were changed, people who were challenged. Denver, the ex-homeless guy "speaks" in several of the chapters. He has that wisdom we all crave - the kind that comes from deep down and is not taught in a seminary class. He strikes me as that guy who uses few words, but when he says something - he SAYS something.

In one of the chapters, he discusses being "led" to help others. He says that's ridiculous and he is tired of people talking about being "led". The Word commands us to help "the least of these", not to wait until we feel led. When we stand before God and He asks how we have served, will we say "Well, I just didn't really feel LED to help others?" That is like saying we do not feel led to take the Sabbath day holy or feel LED to refrain from killing and stealing. It is not really the kind of thing we have an option about - not if we are believers. He talks about how we like to gather and have Bible Studies and Small Groups and Meetings of all kinds so we can LEARN about the Bible. Really, though, we should be DOING!!!

At the same time, we have been doing a devotional from our church about unengaged, unreached people groups. This has spurred conversations in my house about people who live in our town who are unreached. Missions must begin at home. So, we have tried to look for opportunities - little ways really - to serve. Today, we did one such act. A student I know lives with her dad. She wanted to make cupcakes for a special needs boy for his birthday Monday, but casually mentioned they did not have a muffin tin. So, I went to the grocery store to buy the supplies she needed. I planned to buy the aluminum throw-away muffin tins, but turned to the "real" pans just to see. Usually, they are much more expensive at the grocery store. Today - TODAY - the muffin tins - ONLY the muffin tins were on sale for the same price as the throw-away ones. And, there was only ONE muffin tin left. Yes, I got a little lump in my throat. I dropped the items at her doorstep. By the time I got home, a picture was on my Facebook of the loot.

When I got in the car after delivering the items, guy on the radio was talking about how we, as Christians, often have a Fellowship of the Engorged - Christians stuffed with knowledge, but overweight because we are not exercising our faith. We spend lots of time learning what God wants and little time DOING it. He talked about the blessing we receive when we serve more than the person we bless.

Denver was right - I love learning about the Word - Bible Studies absolutely have their place. I do not know to be "led" to serve any more than I need to be "led" feed my children. It should be a part of who I am because of WHOSE I am.

CHALLENGE: I have to go exercise some of this spiritual weight I've gained.....join me!

$\mathcal{D}ay$ 55

Tags in my closet

VERSE: Luke 12: 27: "Consider how the lilies grow. They do not labor or spin. Yet I tell you, not even Solomon in all his splendor was dressed like one of these."

Growing up, we did not have a lot of money. My parents went through a divorce when I was three, and my mom worked hard to provide as a single mom. She re-married when I was five, and we moved to a different state. Within a couple years, there were two little brothers added to the family. Our family had a lot of love, but not necessarily a lot of money. God provided for our our needs - I am not complaining! However, many times I wanted a new Easter dress like the other girls. Mom made my dresses, and I was appreciative. My grandmother often brought a bag of clothes to my house and I picked out items I liked. They were fine and provided something I needed, but I always felt like I was missing a little something. Sometimes I just wanted something with a tag on it... something that was bought specifically for me. I wanted more than a hand-me-down, something second-hand. When I was in high school, I had a job so I could buy clothes for myself and no longer raided the brown paper sacks from my grandmother. As bad as I had to admit it, there were moments of profound insecurity in my situation. Sometimes I just did not feel "good enough". Even today, I always have to maintain at least one item in my closet that still has tags. It is crazy, I know! I love to pull out something new and clip the tags and wear my new frock. When I know it has belonged to only me, there is a comfort in knowing it is mine.

Sometimes, we treat our relationship with God like a hand-me-down relationship and wonder why we are not quite fulfilled. We assume that because our grandmother or parents or our pastor or our friends have a relationship with Christ, we can pick through the parts of that relationship we like and use it as our own. We believe them and count on them to pray for us and often feel like our relationship hinges on their beliefs. However, our relationship with Him must be our own. It must be specifically for us! If I was the only person on earth in need of a Savior, He would have died for me all the same! He loves ME intimately as if I was the only person who needed Him. He loves each of us that much. There is no need for us to look for a hand-me-down Christianity. He designed a relationship with each of us that is specific to our situation, our needs, our dependence on Him. All we have to do is ask Him.

I am glad I have the ability to have a relationship with the Creator of the universe such that He cares about every facet of my life. I do not need to seek my faith in others, in church members, in conferences, in my family, in others I esteem as "more Christian" than me. I seek my faith in HIM because nothing else will satisfy. My life was bought with a price and He stands ready to welcome me into the family!

From the 1890 George Robinson hymn to the modern-day Hillsong anthem, "Oceans," the words ring true: I am His and He is mine!

CHALLENGE: Are you living out your faith as if it were a hand-me-down, something that belonged to someone else? Live your faith as if it had new tags on it - as it were bought JUST for you - because it was! Live with security, knowing He loves YOU and desires a relationship with YOU!

Day 56

I cannot say I trust if I only trust Him when I get what I want

VERSE: Psalm 25:1-2: "To you, O Lord, I lift up my soul; in you I trust, O my God. Do not let me be put to shame, nor let my enemies triumph over me."

A couple years ago, I had a great epiphany. I would pray for God's will for a certain circumstance in my life and then I would outline how I needed God to work out the situation for my benefit. Sometimes, it would even be for the benefit of my friends and family. My prayer life was strong (or so I thought) as I always went to God to ask Him to bless "my" plan. After all, I am sure He needs my input on what is best in my life. The Bible says, "ask and you shall receive" right? I have grown up in the church and knew that God does not always say "yes".

Actually, that is not always true. God does always say, "YES". He always says yes to His will, to what will further the kingdom, to what will continue to weave the tapestry of our lives in a way that we cannot fathom. For my whole life, I have said that I trust Him. But, I found myself wavering in that trust when I did not get a job I wanted, when the pregnancy tests were negative month after month, year after year. My faith was a little shaky when life did not line up exactly how I thought they should, when I got the phone call that my mom's cancer test was positive, when a family divorce brought us to our knees, when some parts of my childhood were far less than wonderful.

If I only trust God when life is going my way, that is not trust at all. Not AT ALL!!!! Treating God like a spiritual Santa Clause is wrong. That is not a Savior - that is a vending machine. Let me push a button (say a little prayer) so I can get what I want (insert prayer here). A Savior is someone I trust every single day. Every.single.day! That means He knows what is best for me, even when I do not. Even when I think I know the right answer, I trust He has the BEST answer. I am a work in progress, but I am learning more and more to trust His will because He always says, "yes" to what is right. A few months ago, we found a house we liked and thought would be perfect for our family. We made an offer and they accepted. The entire time, we prayed. In the end, the deal fell through. I was devastated. We later discovered that there was far more work to be done than we anticipated and that the house required an enormous amount of flood insurance. This time, it was easy to see that God said "yes" to our future by not allowing the deal to come to fruition. Many times, it is not that easy to see God's hand at work. But, I will trust Him. I WILL trust Him. I will TRUST Him. I will trust HIM! And not just when He gives me what I want, but every day, in every way.

CHALLENGE: As we grow in this journey together, I will pray for you and ask that you pray for me as we learn to trust God in everything. Let us stop asking God to simply bless our own plans, but to work out His perfect will in our lives.

Day 57

When you say nothing at all

VERSE: Job 33:14: "For God does speak - now one way, now another, though man may not perceive it."

In most relationships, there is a talker and a listener, right? Well, my husband and I have been married for over 18 years, and anyone who knows us would say that I am the talker and he is the listener. Do not get me wrong, we talk about most everything from the weather to what kind of day we had to the schedule for the boys to our thoughts on the deepest of topics to laughing about silly matters. Somehow he can simply accomplish all that with far fewer words than me.

We were best friends almost instantly in college (I met him my very first day) and started dating two years later. We dated for two years and then got married. Everyone laughed at us because I am definitely the more outgoing one of the two of us. I must confess that he often "says" more than I ever dreamed. He can speak volumes with just a look. He is one of those people that, when he speaks, people listen. In fact, we sang "When you say nothing at all" at our wedding. It was quite appropriate! I remember walking down the aisle and his eyes held forever in them. I could see my future, a secure love, the promise of tomorrow. He said more in those steps than a lifetime could explain. He completely held my gaze without one spoken word.

Isn't God like that? When He speaks, we should listen. It means that there is something significant to be said, for God does not waste His words. Take the Bible for instance. Millions of books have been written about thousands of topics. Yet, His Word stands true for all time. He spoke the words we need to hear. There are also moments in our lives when He speaks to our very souls. We should stay attuned to that still, small voice. For when He speaks, there is something we need to hear.

There are times God does not speak. Those are the times we look around and see His handiwork and know that He still holds forever in His hands. The majesty of nature, the cry of a newborn baby, the frailty of a grandmother's hand before she steps into eternity, the laughter of a child, the smell of jasmine, the touch of a best friend's hand when times are tough, the gaze of a groom as he sees his bride.

As we talk to God through prayer and through mental conversations, we can sometimes become chatty. So chatty we forget to listen. His words may be few, but they are profound.

CHALLENGE: Think about your life right now! What causes you joy? What causes you sorrow? God cares about everything about us. Listen to the still, small voice. Look around you and hear His "words". They say, "I love you!"

Day 58

What IS Missions, really?

VERSE: Matthew 28:19: "Therefore, go and make disciples of all nations, baptizing them in the name of the Father and of the Son and of the Holy Spirit."

Have you ever been on a mission trip? I remember going to camp starting in 2nd grade. Our church did various mission projects for "little old ladies" around town. I went on my first foreign mission trip when I was a senior in high school. We went to Belize to do street ministry and a series of concerts. It was truly life changing. They lost my luggage (which was returned the day before we came home) and I had to wash my one change of clothes everyday and switch back and forth. We did not have hot water or electricity. I had to learn how to take a quick shower and how to style my hair with no devices. I also began to learn to share my faith with strangers and to see past a skeptical nature into someone's heart.

For several years, we traveled a week during the summer to build a church through a local organization, "Builders for Christ". It was an awesome week of shooting a nail gun, popping chalk lines, and setting rafters. My husband traveled to Mexico to build a chapel, and even learned a few Spanish words. We have served at church in various capacities ranging from providing food for D-Now to working at Egg-citement to Sunday School projects to purchasing gifts for a Christmas family. Last year on Christmas Day, our family engaged in Random Acts of Christmas Kindness (RACKs) and took treats to the fire houses and those working at gas stations and hospitals. These events are all missions, right?

They are indeed. I was reminded this week of what missions is really all about. We have a young man at our school that has had a rough time in life as he has lost all but one significant person in his life. Many people have tried to help him, but it sometimes seems not to matter. He is like a bull in a china shop some days. There are times, it is tiresome. He asked to spend some time with a teacher over our spring break. Any person in their right mind would find themselves too busy. She did not. She picked him up, took him to see his frail grandmother in another city, bought him some clothes so he would have some articles without holes in them, took him to see a movie, and even taught him some about home improvements. I chatted with her a couple times and told her it was twelve hours of missions.

That is exactly what it was! Missions!!! By definition, "missions" is an act carried out to spread the faith. What could possibly spread the faith more than demonstrating care and concern over another human being? When we return to school next week, I expect that this young man will still have his moments of immaturity. I also expect that seeds have been planted and watered because he has seen Love in Action. What could possibly be mission-minded than that? I am excited to see what the future holds for him. Truthfully, we all learned some lessons from this precious teacher. She has encouraged us to step up to the plate and demonstrate love and not just speak words of belief.

She is truly the epitome of a missionary!

CHALLENGE: Look around and see needs of others - not just those on the surface, but those lying underneath. Showing Love in Action is the essence of missions. Find a way to minister to someone today. It is not necessary to go across the ocean to be a missionary - just across the street.

Day 59

Jealousy....the Green-eyed Monster

VERSE: Proverbs 27:4: "Anger is cruel and fury overwhelming, but who can stand before jealousy?"

Recently, I worked hard to lose a few pounds. For many years, I have enjoyed running as a hobby. The problem is, I also enjoy eating as a hobby. As the stresses of being a wife, mother, employee, friend, church member mounted, I began to eat for comfort. I still ran, but not in proportion to my food. My intake was more than my outgo. For months, I whined about it and was discouraged each morning when I stepped in my closet and had to breathe in a little deeper to button the pants.

One day, I decided to do something about it. For four months, I worked and counted calories and stopped having cereal right before bedtime and wrote down what I ate. Ultimately, I was able to get back to the healthy size I was looking for. One day, I was chatting with a friend and she said, "I'm jealous". Immediately, I shot back, "Well, it's okay because I have always been jealous of you - you have awesome hair and the cutest shoes of anyone I know." We are great friends and this really was silly banter. But, it made me think.

Jealousy is when we count someone else's blessings. It is when we look at someone else's life through our own lens and assume they have it so much better than we do. Have you been there? I know I have. We look at someone's house or their vacations or their relationship with their family or their career or their children or their artistic ability or their charisma and we get jealous. We see the best feature in each person we know and wish we had all of their talents and high points. If we let that fester, it will devour us with negativity. We do not count their troubles, just their blessings. What we often fail to realize is that people are jealous of us - they are counting our blessings.

This is a travesty on both parts! God has called us to count OUR blessings, not someone else's. His blessings for us are unique to us because they are exactly what we need. The same is true for those we are watching. When we skim over our own blessings and pout because we do not have the blessings others have, it is almost like a slap in the face of God to say, "that's not good enough". If my children treated were not appreciative of what they received, it would grieve my heart. How much more, then, does it grieve the heart of God when we treat our blessings - the ones He has bestowed on us - so carelessly?

CHALLENGE: Write down 10 of your blessings. Yes, write the major ones - salvation, family, health. Be more specific, though. What has God blessed you with that you take for granted?

Day 60

Ulterior Motives

VERSE: Proverbs 21:2: "All a man's ways seem right to him, but The Lord weighs the heart."

During the season of Lent, many people across the world give up something of substance and focus that time or money on eternal matters. Growing up, I was largely unaware of the Lenten season and the significance in the celebrations. However, in my adult life, I have seen great value in sacrificing for God and for carving out specific time to focus on Him. This year a dear friend of mine flipped the script and decided to ADD something everyday during Lent. She performed a random act of kindness for people each day. I was simply amazed at how attuned she is to people and their needs. She bought house shoes for a lady, took homemade macaroni and cheese to a sick friend, brought silver shoes to someone who needed some dancing shoes, etc. It was simply amazing - as is she! She was telling me about one particular day when she took breakfast to an office in our district. She met one of the ladies in a parking lot to deliver the goods. Later she mentioned she needed some information from this lady and she bet that breakfast would expedite her answers. We laughed as I jokingly told her that breakfast did not count if she had ulterior motives. She gave me a hard time, and we moved on about our day.

Except, I kept thinking about it. How many times have I done something nice for someone, but with a hint of ulterior motive? How many times have I gone out of my to act like I cared only hoping to receive something in return? I remember many years ago doing a Bible Study with a group of ladies in Louisiana. I was very proud of myself one day because I had gone out of my way to take a pie to a needy friend. I was quite pleased with myself for my sacrificial giving. I told the ladies at the Bible Study all about it. Half way into the story, I realized I had taken the pie for all the wrong reasons. It was for my glory, for my benefit. There are many times I do the right thing for the wrong reasons. Sometimes I do good deeds for my own gain. When I do, my reward is shallow and fleeting.

We are human, and sometimes we do godly efforts for human purposes. The true mark of growing in maturity in our Christian faith is when we act on our faith with pure motives. This is a matter of the heart. I do believe this is why God says that obedience is better than sacrifice. Sometimes we can sacrifice but stay in control. It can still be for own glory. Obedience means we hand over control to God. That takes away ulterior motives and selfishness on our part. Obedience is hard, but so worth it in the end.

Maybe for Lent, and everyday, I will give up my motives for His desires. I will focus on obedience!

CHALLENGE: Take inventory of the last five acts of kindness you performed. Were they for your benefit? Be honest!

Day 61

A review of Faith

VERSE: 2 Corinthians 5:7: "We live by faith, not by sight."

I am part of a women's Sunday School class. Over the past three months, we have studied the lives of those listed in the Great Hall of Faith found in Hebrews 11. It is an amazing chapter filled with lives of sinners and knuckleheads just like me. It is also an amazing chapter filled with lives that were touched by the master to change the course of history. Here is a synopsis:

- Abel offered a better sacrifice
- Enoch was whisked away
- Noah warned of things not yet seen
- Abraham obeyed
- Sarah laughed and longed for a city beyond what she knew
- Isaac accepted God's plan
- Jacob wrestled and finished well
- Joseph was unwavering and was concerned about his bones
- Moses made a huge impact from the Burning Bush to the Red Sea and beyond, but didn't really start his ministry until age 80
- Joshua marched around the walls and blew a trumpet
- Rahab was the unlikely prostitute who hid the spies

Faith is relational, based on God's character, and steeped in the fact of the truth of the resurrection. Faith is confident assurance that

God is in control and that He has something better planned for us than we could ever imagine. The word faith originates from the Latin word "fides" meaning promise, assurance, word of honor. Faith is not religion, wishful thinking, mysterious optimism, or positive thinking.

The faith of the Christian is forgetting what we think we see from our perspective and holding on to what we know to be true, based on the promises in the Word. As we walk the pathway of this life and face the struggles thrown our way, take heart from the great heroes of the faith. They were not perfect, but had faith that God's way was better than their own.

CHALLENGE: How do you view faith? Do you view faith as spiritually crossing your fingers that circumstances will turn out okay, or do you trust that God's will is higher than your own?

Day 62

What a difference a day makes

VERSE: John 14:27: "Peace I leave with you; my peace I give you. I do not give to you as the world gives. Do not let your hearts be troubled and do not be afraid."

As of today, I have been on this earth for 14,915 days. Most of those days have been pretty boring, to be honest. Most days have a basic ebb and flow and are not necessarily life-altering. However, there are some days that have taken me to the tip of the mountaintop and some days that have rocked me to the very core of my being. Throughout my some odd 15,000 days (some a little more odd than others), I have learned a few lessons along the way.

I have learned that life is not always fair and I have learned that having encouraging people around you is one of life's biggest blessings and I have learned there are big lessons in everyday happenings and I have learned that I am not too good to go through a hard time. I have learned that God is good all the time and that my attitude is the one thing that I can control. I have learned that there is joy in the little things and that what truly make me happy are not "things" at all.

There are days that have had a profound impact on my life, many of those days have been shared within these covers. However, there are other days that have made me who I am today. Some of those days are very dark and kept tucked away in a private place in my heart. Some of those days brought so much excitement that there are no adequate words to describe! What is constant is God's faithfulness. He is the steady, the true calm in my storm, the anchor that holds me.

The day that made the MOST difference was when I invited Jesus into my heart. I went from knowing about Him to knowing Him intimately. That was the day that secured my salvation, my place in heaven. It was also the day that gave me purpose and a meaning beyond the temporal. If you have not had such a day in your life, I pray you seek Him through His word in the book of John. Taste and see that The Lord, He is good! This is one decision you will never regret.

My prayer is, as we wind down sixty-two days of learning about an extraordinary God in an ordinary life, that one of these days has touched you in a meaningful way. God has whispered to me throughout my life an I hope you have overheard some of those whispers through the words on these pages. Some days have been life-changing and some have been life-saving. Life is a journey, and I appreciate you stopping in with me to walk by my side. We will each continue on through everyday life, through the ebb and flow. I pray you have been encouraged to walk closer to His side, to seek His face, and to see Him in the everyday. For, that is where He dwells and whispers our name.

Thank you for sharing with me. Thank you for listening to His words, and for seeing yourself in a different light. Listen to the still, small voice for it is true.....one day can make all the difference!

CHALLENGE: Listen for His voice. Seek His face. Everyday.